Duesenberg Aircraft Engines

A Technical Description

Duesenberg Aircraft Engines

A Technical Description

William Pearce

Old Machine Press
Los Osos, CA
www.oldmachinepress.com

Copyright © 2012 William Pearce

All rights reserved.

The information in this work is true and complete to the best of our knowledge. However, all information is presented without any guarantee on the part of the Author or Publisher, who also disclaim any liability incurred in connection with the use of the information.

All trademarks, trade names, model names and numbers, and other product designations referred to herein are the property of their respective owners and are used solely for identification purposes. This work is a publication of Old Machine Press and has not been licensed, approved, sponsored, or endorsed by any other person or entity.

ISBN 978-0-9850353-0-3

Revision 20150122a

On the cover:
Upper left—Rear view of the Duesenberg V-12 aircraft engine.
Middle left—The 16-valve, four-cylinder Duesenberg aircraft engine.
Lower left—Sectional end view of the Duesenberg-built King-Bugatti aircraft engine.
Right—Rear view of the Duesenberg Model H aircraft engine (Martt Clupper photo via AirPigz, www.airpigz.com).

Tittle page:
The Gallaudet D-1: perhaps the first aircraft to fly with Duesenberg engines.

Back cover:
Front end view and sectional of the Duesenberg Model H aircraft engine.

Humble beginnings.
Young Fred and Augie Duesenberg on their racing bicycles.

Duesenberg wartime ad from 1918.

Contents

Preface	1
1. Fred and Augie Duesenberg	3
2. Duesenberg "Walking Beam" Valve Gear	9
3. Straight-Four Engine of 1915	13
4. V-12 Engine of 1916	19
5. Sixteen-Valve Straight-Four Engine	29
6. The King-Bugatti U-16 Engine	43
7. Duesenberg Model H V-16 Engine	57
Epilogue	81
Appendix A – Duesenberg Aircraft Engine Comparison	83
Appendix B – Duesenberg Valve Gear Patent	85
Appendix C – The King V-12 Aero Engine	95
Appendix D – Duesenberg Engine Test House	99
Appendix E – Christensen Self-Starter	103
Appendix F – Notes on Descriptions and Conflicting Information	107
Bibliography	111

Preface

This book began as a quest to consolidate information on the Duesenberg Model H aircraft engine and eventually evolved to include all the Duesenberg aircraft engines. Information on these engines is hard to come by, for while the Duesenberg automobile became legendary, Duesenberg aircraft engines did not advance aviation or even the art of aircraft engines. But these engines did possess unique features and are well worth being remembered.

My interest in the Duesenberg Model H began as a result of Martt Clupper's article on the engine. I found the article on his website, www.airpigz.com, and the photos in his article made me want to know more about this masterpiece of an engine from a bygone era.

My internet searches did not uncover much more than what I had already read about the engine. I turned to my ever-expanding bookshelf, and I went through several engine books from the 1920s. I found much more information on the Model H, but to my dismay, I also found contradictions and closed the books with many questions unanswered. That was when I decided to get serious with my research and to put together all I could find on the Model H. I knew others were interested in this engine and that it would be very helpful to have most of the information in one place. I soon realized that the Model H owed much to the previous Duesenberg aircraft engines, so I included them as part of its history. While searching for more about these earlier engines, I realized that information on them was even harder to find, so I decided to include everything I could on all the Duesenberg designed or manufactured aircraft engines.

Admittedly, everything contained in this work exists in print somewhere else. Even so, I'm confident that much of the information will be new to the reader, given the rarity of the subject. I have compiled the information from old and obscure sources, and I attempted to clarify descriptions and contradictory information (see Appendix F). I have done my best to make sure the information is complete and correct; any errors or omissions are entirely my own.

I would like to thank Martt Clupper for his photos and story of the Duesenberg Model H, which were the catalyst for this work; the *Aircraft Engine Historical Society* (www.enginehistory.com) for everything they do; Tom Fey and Kim McCutcheon for their valuable and appreciated advice; and my wife, Katie, for her hard work helping me edit this book.

William Pearce
oldmachinepress@gmail.com
January 2012

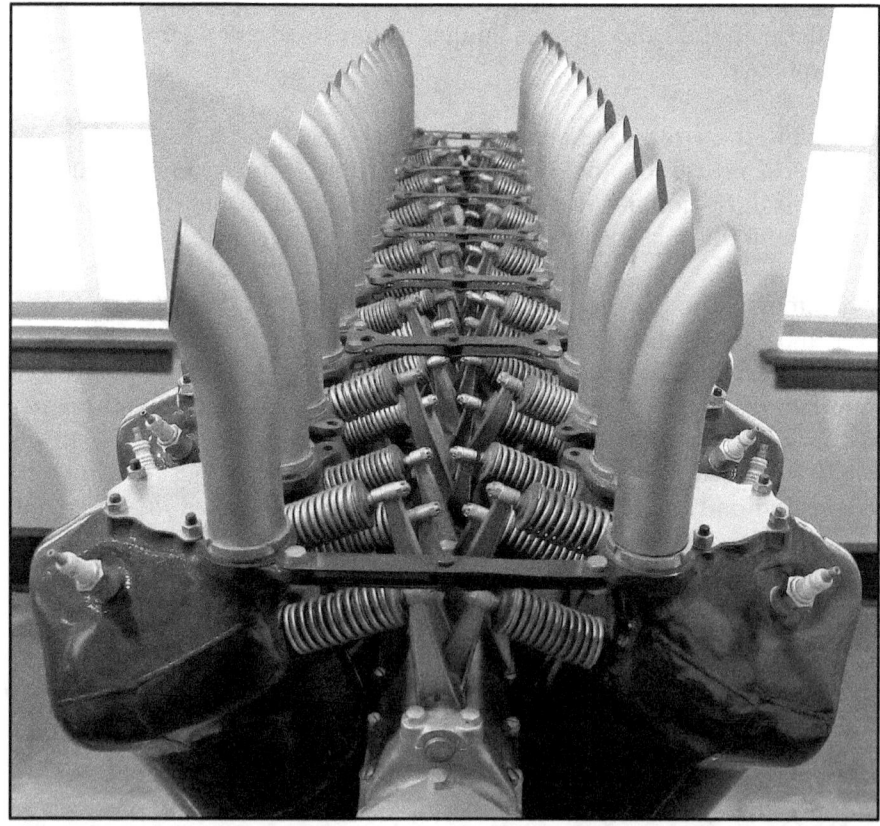

The image that started my quest: the complicated Vee of the Duesenberg Model H aircraft engine (Martt Clupper photo via AirPigz, www.airpigz.com).

1. Fred and Augie Duesenberg

Frederick and August Duesenberg were born in Kirchheide, Germany, Frederick on December 6, 1876 and August on December 12, 1879. In 1885, they immigrated to the United States with their mother and other siblings. They joined their older brother, already in the U.S., and settled in Rockford, Iowa. Fred began building and racing bicycles with Augie as his able assistant. While the self-taught engineers shared their talents, Fred was more of the genius designer, and Augie was the fabricator who brought the designs to life. The brothers' interest in bicycles soon shifted to building and racing motorcycles. By the late 1890, both brothers were operating bicycle and motorcycle repair shops, Fred still in Rockford, and Augie 40 miles away in Garner, Iowa.

Augie (left) and Fred (right) Duesenberg in the 1920s.

In the early 1900s, Fred turned his focus to the automobile and moved to Kenosha, Wisconsin to work as a mechanic and test driver on the Rambler automobile, produced by the Thomas B. Jeffery Company. In 1902, the

Thomas B. Jeffery Company was the second largest automobile manufacturer in the world.

But Fred had greater aspirations and returned home in 1904. Together, he and Augie set up a shop in Des Moines, Iowa and began building their first automobile, known as the Marvel. Powered by a 24 hp, two-cylinder engine of their own design, the auto caught the eye of Edward Mason, a local attorney, who provided funding for its production. Now known as the Mason Runabout, the vehicle made its commercial debut in 1906 and was marketed as the fastest and strongest two-cylinder car in America. The Mason Runabout was the start of these mechanically gifted brothers making a name for themselves building autos and engines that were considered some of the very best of their time.

Fred Maytag, of washing machine fame, bought 60 percent of the Mason Automobile Company in 1910. The company was renamed the Maytag-Mason Motor Company and moved to Waterloo, Iowa. Maytag quickly lost interest in automobile manufacturing, and Mason moved the brothers back to Des Moines, where they worked out of a garage at a car dealership. In 1912, Mason supported the brothers' auto racing endeavors.

In 1913, the Duesenberg brothers founded the Duesenberg Motor Company, Inc. in St. Paul, Minnesota to build race engines and cars under their own name. Fred and Augie became famous designing and building racing engines for automobiles and boats, and the Duesenberg name went on to become a legend.

Before he was America's top scoring ace of World War I, Eddie Rickenbacker was a manager and a race car driver for the Duesenberg Company. In 1914, Rickenbacker drove a Duesenberg to a 10th place finish in the Indianapolis 500, with another Duesenberg finishing 12th. By 1916, it was estimated that 60 percent of race cars were powered by Duesenberg engines, a rather inconceivable figure.

In early 1917, Duesenberg Motor Company and the Loew-Victor Engine Company combined to form the Duesenberg Motors Corporation. The new corporation concentrated on manufacturing engines for marine, auto, and aviation use. At the time, Loew-Victor Co. was producing Fred Duesenberg designed high-speed marine engines and had the experience and equipment to produce other Duesenberg engines. The new company was headquartered in New York City, New York, but production took place in Elizabeth, New Jersey. In May of 1918, the Duesenberg Corporation completed construction of a state-of-the-art engine test house next to their plant in Elizabeth, NJ. This test house was believed to be the world's largest engine test house at the time (see Appendix D).

Eddie Rickenbacker in his Duesenberg Indianapolis 500 racer for 1914.

At the end of World War I, Duesenberg ceased building aviation and marine engines. The company was again reorganized, and the facilities in New Jersey were sold. In 1920, the Duesenberg Automobile and Motors Company, Inc. was founded with a new headquarters and factory in Indianapolis, Indiana. Fred and Augie Duesenberg were now focused on the production of passenger cars, their new straight-eight engine, and building racing cars and engines. Duesenberg's first passenger car, the Model A, went into production in 1921.

Tommy Milton running at Daytona Beach in 1920 where he recorded a run of 156.046 mph in the twin straight-eight powered Duesenberg.

In the 1920s the Duesenberg automobile really hit its stride. At Tommy Milton's suggestion, the brothers built a car around two straight-eight Duesenberg engines. On April 27, 1920, Milton drove the twin-engined Duesenberg at Daytona Beach, Florida and set the American land speed record at 156.046 mph. The record stood until 1927. Duesenberg autos won seven of the top ten places at Indy in 1920; Le Mans in 1921; and Indy in 1922 (powered by a Miller engine), 1924, 1925, and 1927. During this time period Duesenberg introduced a centrifugal supercharger for its straight-eight engine, with the help of Dr. Sanford A. Moss, and numerous records were set by Duesenberg-powered machines.

Jimmy Murphy was the first American to win the French Grand Prix at Le Mans and did so at the wheel of a Duesenberg in 1921.

Unfortunately, the brothers were better engineers than businessmen, and the Duesenberg Automobile and Motors Company was in need of financial rescue; this rescue came in the form of Errett Lobban Cord, of the Cord Company, in 1926. Fred, now serving as Vice President of Duesenberg Inc., went on to design the Duesenberg Model J. Considered the epitome of the Duesenberg line, the Model J was built from 1928 to 1937. Sadly, Duesenberg and its Cord Company parent declined in the 1930s and went out of business in 1937.

Fred Duesenberg passed away on July 26, 1932, before the company that bore his name declined. He died of complications from injuries he suffered in an automobile accident on July 2, 1932. Fred was 55 years old and still considered to be very much in his prime.

Augie continued to work his magic as a designer and mechanic, aiding several successful speed record attempts. The pinnacle of Augie's post-Duesenberg career was designing and building Ab Jenkins' Curtiss Conqueror powered *Mormon Meteor III* that Jenkins drove to 26 endurance speed records, some of which still stand today. After World War II, Augie attempted to bring back the Duesenberg automobile, but to no avail. He passed away from a heart attack on January 18, 1955.

Ab Jenkins (left) shakes hands with Augie Duesenberg (right) in front of the Curtiss Conqueror (V-1570) powered Mormon Meteor III *at the Indianapolis Speedway in 1938.*

Today, Duesenberg autos are sought after by classic car collectors and fetch millions on the auction block; they are the absolute pinnacle of American luxury from the 1920s and 1930s. In August 2011, the very special 1931 Model J Whitell Coupe sold for $10.34 million at Pebble Beach, California, a record for an American car at auction.

Although the Duesenberg auto is famous, their aircraft engines are relatively unknown. In 1915, aviation was in its exciting infancy and war was spreading across Europe. It was clear that the airplane would play a part in the war and an even larger role in transportation. In those days more than ever, the engine was the heart of the aircraft. It was in this dynamic time that the Duesenbergs turned their attention and expertise to aircraft engines, with Fred leading the design and development.

Duesenberg Eddie Rickenbacker ad from 1918; note the "Rickenbacher" spelling. Eddie began spelling his last name "Rickenbacker" in 1914 and used that spelling full time during WWI. He said it was to take the "Hun" out of his name.

2. Duesenberg "Walking Beam" Valve Gear

One of the most unique characteristics of the early Duesenberg engines was their valve gear. Fred and Augie Duesenberg began designing this valve gear in 1910, and it was originally described in their *Internal Combustion Engine* patent application of April 1913. However, in August 1914 the valve gear was divided from the original patent and filed separately, being granted United States patent 1,244,481 in October 1917 (see Appendix B). In the *Valve Gear* patent, Fred and Augie Duesenberg cited the improvements of their valve system for use in internal combustion engines over the inefficiencies of then-current valve systems in use. They claimed that standard valve systems seated poorly, were prone to sticking open due to heat and lack of lubrication, and resulted in poor combustion.

The Duesenberg valve gear used horizontal valves that were perpendicular to the cylinder axis and opened into a small, rectangular clearance space above the cylinders. This space extended the combustion chamber above the piston and ran parallel with the crankshaft. The spark plug was positioned on the opposite side of this space to achieve near instant ignition of the air/fuel mixture, resulting in improved combustion and efficiency. In essence, this configuration gave a stratified charge to the cylinder. The rich air/fuel mixture was ignited by the spark plug positioned near the intake valve in the small combustion space. The flame front then propagated down to the areas of leaner air/fuel mixture throughout the rest of the combustion chamber.

The cylinders and head were a single casting, and large, threaded, removable plugs were inserted into ports opposite the valves in the small combustion chamber space. Once the plugs were removed, the intake and exhaust valves could be inserted or removed through these ports. In addition, the ports allowed the inspection and cleaning of the cylinders and piston crown.

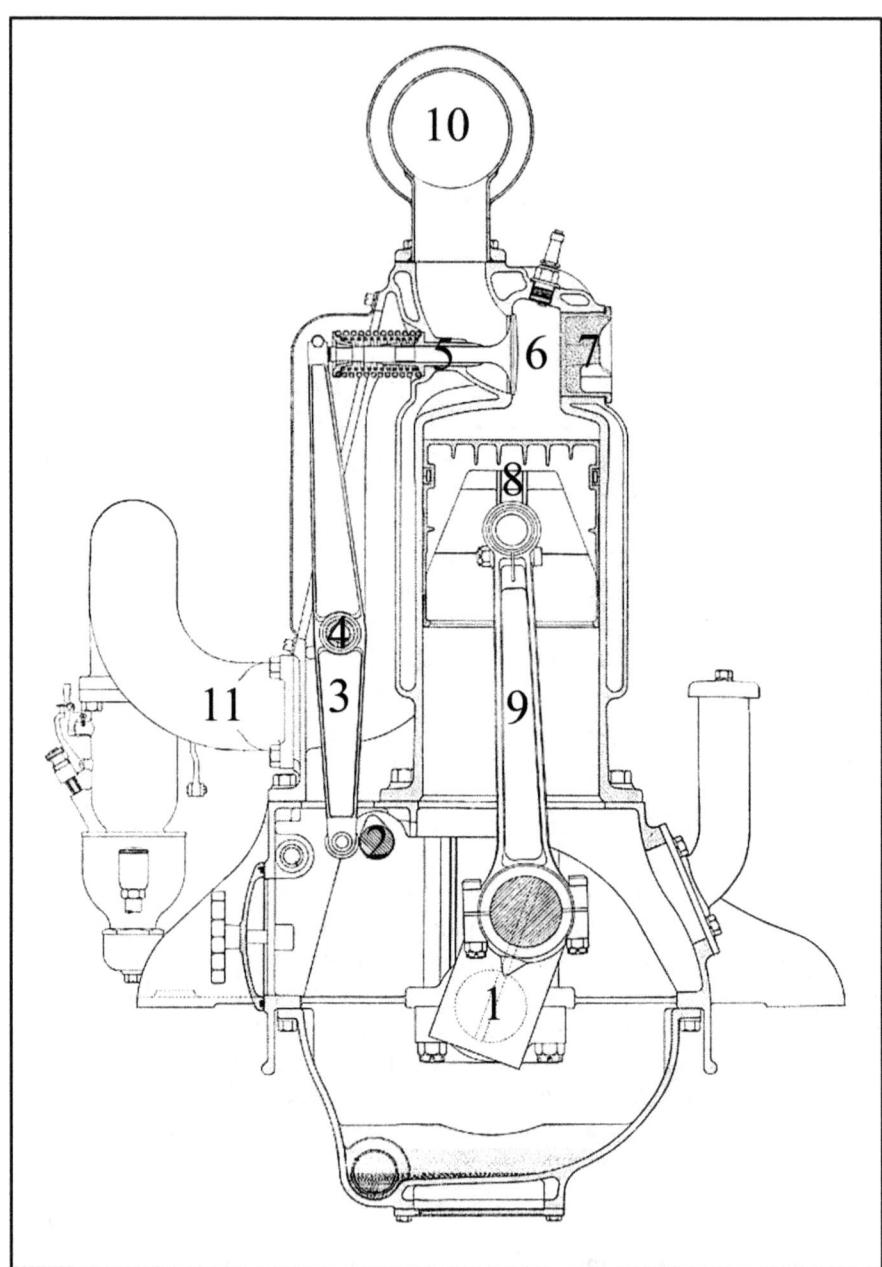

Sectional view of a late model Duesenberg walking beam engine: 1) crankshaft, 2) camshaft, 3) walking beam rocker arm, 4) rocker arm pivot shaft, 5) valve, 6) small combustion space above the piston, 7) threaded port that allowed the removal of the valve, 8) piston, 9) connecting rod, 10) exhaust manifold, 11) intake manifold.

The valves were actuated by very long and large rocker arms, colloquially referred to as "walking beams." The rocker arms were actuated directly by a camshaft running along the engine block. A hardened contact or roller was attached to the rocker arm where it came into contact with the camshaft. The rocker arms were mounted on a common shaft that ran the length of the cylinder block. Each rocker arm was offset on this shaft, creating a short side of the rocker arm and a long side. The short side of the rocker arm was actuated by the camshaft, and the long side of the arm actuated the valve. Camshaft movement on the short side was effectively multiplied on the long side. This enabled the valves to be opened and closed instantly. Due to the length of the rocker arm, the push on the valve was basically a straight line with little side thrust. The entire valve gear could be enclosed; this not only aided in proper lubrication but also protected the valve gear and made it quieter.

The term "walking beams" comes from the visually similar walking beam drilling and pumping machinery first used in the 1800s, predominantly on oil rigs. In addition, many paddle wheel steamboats from the United States were powered by walking beam engines, first introduced in the 1830s.

The Duesenbergs asserted that their valve gear was more reliable, durable, and efficient than the other systems in use at the time. The valves seated better and allowed more efficient combustion. The entire valve gear received good lubrication that reduced wear and heat, subsequently increasing the life of the parts. At a time when exposed valves lubricated by grease cups were the norm, it is easy to see how the Duesenberg valve gear was a definite step forward. The walking beam side valves were used on all the Duesenberg-designed aircraft engines.

By the early 1920s, Fred and Augie Duesenberg had moved on to a more conventional overhead camshaft valve gear. They sold the walking beam engine production rights to the Rochester Motors Corporation of Rochester, New York.

Duesenberg Airplane Engines

THE Duesenberg Airplane Engine is not an automobile motor. It is an engine designed and built to meet the requirements of the Airplane with a very lively understanding of the difficulties to be overcome. It is in no way experimental, as all the dominant features of its design have been worked out and tried out in racing tests on the automobile racing tracks and in motor boat racing. The facts brought out in these fierce tests have been incorporated in this Airplane Engine, making it the simplest and most efficient motor for Aeronautical purposes. A motor that is powerful for its weight, simple in its construction and free from freakish whims in its design. Write to-day for a descriptive bulletin.

DUESENBERG MOTORS CORPORATION, 120 BROADWAY, NEW YORK CITY

Duesenberg airplane engine ad from 1917.

3. Straight-Four Engine of 1915

In 1915, The Duesenberg brothers began to market their engines to power aircraft. The first aircraft engines were slightly modified and lightened versions of the brothers' automotive engines. The aircraft engines were known as the Special A and the Special A3; they differed only in their cylinder bore. Both were water-cooled, inline, monobloc, four-cylinder engines with two valves per cylinder.

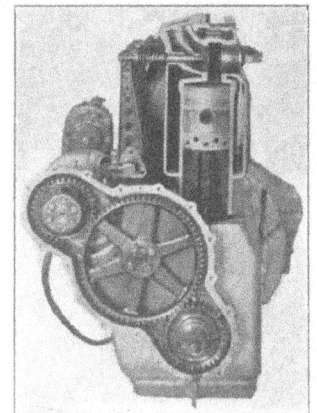

THE DUESENBERG MOTORS

OFFER THESE ADVANTAGES

Valves in the head and an enclosed valve mechanism which is "fool-proof."

Simplicity and compactness.

They hold many records in automobile races.

TWO MODELS

Special A.
Bore 3 63/64 inches
Stroke 6 inches

Special A3
Bore 4 3/8 inches
Stroke 6 inches

We are in a position to make early deliveries

THE DUESENBERG MOTOR COMPANY 2654 University Ave. ST. PAUL, MINN.

Duesenberg ad for the Special A and Special A3 engines from the May 15, 1915 edition of Aerial Age Weekly.

The Special A was the smaller of the two engines. It had an odd size bore of 3 63/64" and a stroke of 6". Total displacement for the Special A was 299 in^3—62 in^3 less than the Special A3. Unfortunately, no reliable power figures have been found for this engine, but given the smaller displacement, it can be assumed that the Special A was less powerful than the Special A3 noted below.

With a 4 3/8" bore and 6" stroke, the larger Special A3 had a total displacement of 361 in^3, and produced 70 hp at 1,500 rpm, 80 hp at 2,000 rpm, and 85 hp at 2,220 rpm. It was claimed to achieve maximum power at 2,500 rpm, but no value has been found. However, most sources rate the engine at 70 hp because 1,500 rpm was the most effective rpm setting for this direct drive engine in an age of fixed-pitch propellers.

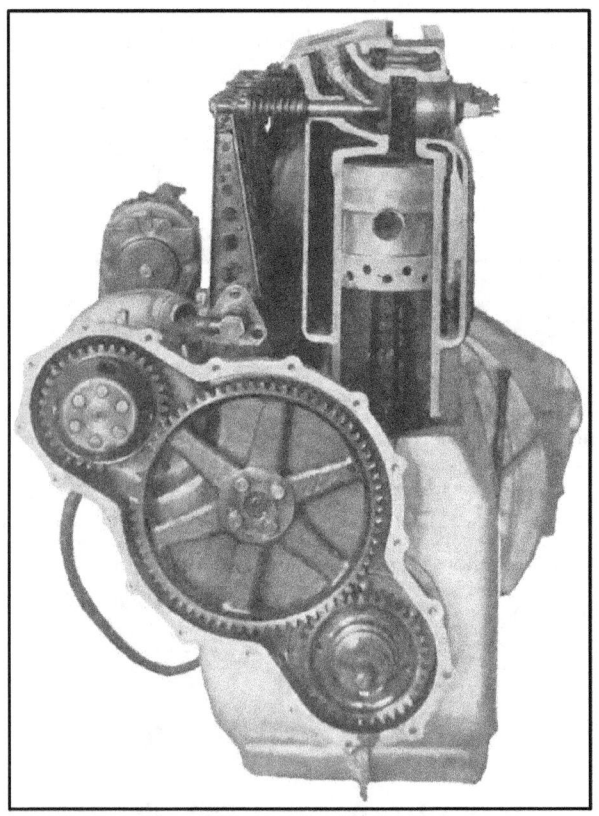

An image that accompanied articles and ads in 1915 detailing the Special A engine series. The cutaway engine provides a good view of the valve, combustion chamber space, and the long walking beam rocker arms. The exposed valve is an exhaust valve. Note the spark plugs located in the removable plugs opposite the valves and the lightening holes drilled through the piston skirt.

Weighing 365 lb, both engines featured the Duesenberg walking beam valve gear, with horizontal valves located in a small space above the piston. Each valve in each cylinder had a large, threaded, removable plug opposite the valve port to provide access for the insertion and removal of the valve. This Duesenberg feature would be used on future aircraft engines as well. Each plug had a hole center-bored and tapped to accept a spark plug.

3. Straight-Four Engine of 1915

The tungsten valves were 2 3/16" in diameter, had a 2 1/16" throat diameter, and a lift of 3/8". Exhaust was expelled from the top of the engine from ports above the exhaust valves. The center two cylinders had their exhaust ports paired. The intake valves for adjacent cylinders were located together so that the first two cylinders shared an intake runner, and the last two cylinders shared an intake runner. These two runners were cast integral with the side of the engine block, between the cylinders and the rocker arms. The runners joined together at the middle of the engine to form a single intake that began at the engine's side. Here, a manifold was attached to the outside of the engine to enable the use of a single updraft carburetor.

A Duesenberg auto racing engine very similar to the Special A and Special A3. Of note are the long walking beam rocker arms and the intake runners cast integral with the block. The small manifold below the rocker arms is where the carburetor would attach to feed the intake runners that led to the cylinders.

Long walking beam rocker arms actuated the valves and were made of pressed steel with welded and hardened contacts that ran directly on the camshaft. The camshaft had a large gear bolted to it and was driven by the crankshaft. This large gear had twice the teeth of the crankshaft pinion, achieving the required speed reduction of the camshaft—half that of the crankshaft.

The pistons were ribbed on their undersides to transfer heat away from their crowns. This ribbing also added strength and stiffness. Only one piston ring was used, and it was made up of three pieces, another unique characteristic of Duesenberg engines. Holes were drilled in the piston skirt to make it lighter. The wrist pin was 1 1/4" in diameter, was clamped by the upper end of the connecting rod, and had its bearing in the piston. The wrist pins were bored out and tapered to the outer ends to achieve maximum strength but minimum weight. They were case hardened, ground, and then polished. The connecting rods were 12" long and made from heat treated chrome-nickel steel of I-beam construction. The rod was held to the crankshaft by four 7/16" vanadium steel bolts.

Side view of the Special A with the two throw crankshaft visible through the removed inspection cover. The panel removed from the cylinder block made up the water jacket.

The 2 1/4" crankshaft was made from chrome-nickel steel and supported by two bearings, one in the front of the engine and the other in the rear. The front bearing was 4" long, and the rear was 4 1/2". The two center cylinders were on the same throw, which was 180° from the first and fourth cylinders. The connecting rod bearings were 2 1/2" long and 2 1/4" in diameter.

The engines used a combination of pressure and splash lubrication. Oil was pressure fed directly to all bearings and to the rocker arm pivot shaft. The connecting rods, cylinders, and valves used splash lubrication. Two oil pumps were utilized. The first pump supplied oil directly from the main oil tank to the bearings. From the bearings, the oil drained into troughs under the connecting rods for splash lubrication. The second oil pump was larger and took oil from the troughs and returned it to the tank.

The two spark plugs per cylinder were fired by a Bosch magneto, and fuel was provided by a Harry A. Miller Manufacturing Company (Miller) carburetor. The crankcase was of the barrel type and had a 6" by 18" access cover on each side.

Engine Specifications

Engine:	Special A
First Run:	1915
Type:	Straight 4-cylinder, two valves per cylinder, water-cooled, aircraft engine
Displacement:	299 in^3
Bore:	3.984375"
Stroke:	6"
Gear Reduction:	None
Carburetion:	One Miller updraft
Weight:	365 lb

Engine:	Special A3
First Run:	1915
Type:	Straight 4-cylinder, two valves per cylinder, water-cooled, aircraft engine
Horsepower:	70 hp at 1,500 rpm, 85 hp at 2,220 rpm
Displacement:	361 in^3
Bore:	4.375"
Stroke:	6"
BMEP:	102.4 psi at 1,500 rpm, 84.0 psi at 2,220 rpm
Specific Weight:	5.21 lb/hp at 1,500 rpm, 4.29 lb/hp at 2,220 rpm
Specific Power:	0.19 hp/in^3 at 1,500 rpm, 0.24 hp/in^3 at 2,220 rpm
Gear Reduction:	None
Carburetion:	One Miller updraft
Weight:	365 lb

Duesenberg Motors

Announcement!

Duesenberg Motors Corporation has been organized to manufacture Aeroplane, Marine and Automobile Motors for those who can afford and demand the best.

EACH of the three types of motors will be built on the same general design, differing only enough to adapt them to their individual requirements. The Duesenberg Design has proven itself in actual service for a number of years.

> Duesenberg Motors are installed in Seaplanes now in the Service of the United States Navy.
>
> Duesenberg Motors were installed in the first motor boat to make a mile-a-minute speed.
>
> Duesenberg Motors were installed in the boat that won the Displacement Runabout Classic at the Miami Regatta this year.
>
> More than 60% of all racing cars on American Speedways in 1916 were equipt with Duesenberg Motors.

The Duesenberg Aeroplane Motor, a sixteen valve, four cylinder, 125 H. P. engine, typifies the evolution of the Duesenberg Design which has passed through the severe test of automobile and motor boat racing. It now occupies a dominant position in the field of internal combustion engine design.

The racing experience has refined this design to a hitherto unattained degree. It has made it possible to build an engine developing 1 H. P. for every 3.5 cubic inches piston displacement. Furthermore, this motor only weighs 3.5 lbs. to the H. P. and is probably the most compact aeroplane engine of its power in existence.

Duesenberg Aeroplane Motors have proven themselves in actual service. The United States Navy is using them in the Gallaudet Seaplanes. The Lanzius Changeable Angle of Incidence Airplanes also use this powerful motor as standard equipment.

A very interesting bulletin has been prepared on this Aeroplane Motor in which complete data is given in conjunction with full illustrations. Write or telephone for a copy today.

Duesenberg Motors Corporation
120 Broadway, New York City

Duesenberg Motors announcement of its reorganization from May 1917. Detailed in the announcement are the 16-valve, four-cylinder engine; the Gallaudet D-1 seaplane; and the Lanzius L1 biplane with a drawing (see section 5. Sixteen-Valve Straight-Four Engine on page 29).

4. V-12 Engine of 1916

In 1916, Duesenberg went big with the creation of a V-12 aircraft engine, which was one of the largest aircraft engines at the time. Duesenberg had previous experience with large engines, having built a 3,221 in^3 straight 12-cylinder marine engine in 1914. Overall, construction of the aircraft engine was similar to the 1915 four-cylinder aircraft engine, but much of the engine's form came from marine engines designed by Fred Duesenberg and built by the Loew-Victor Engine Company.

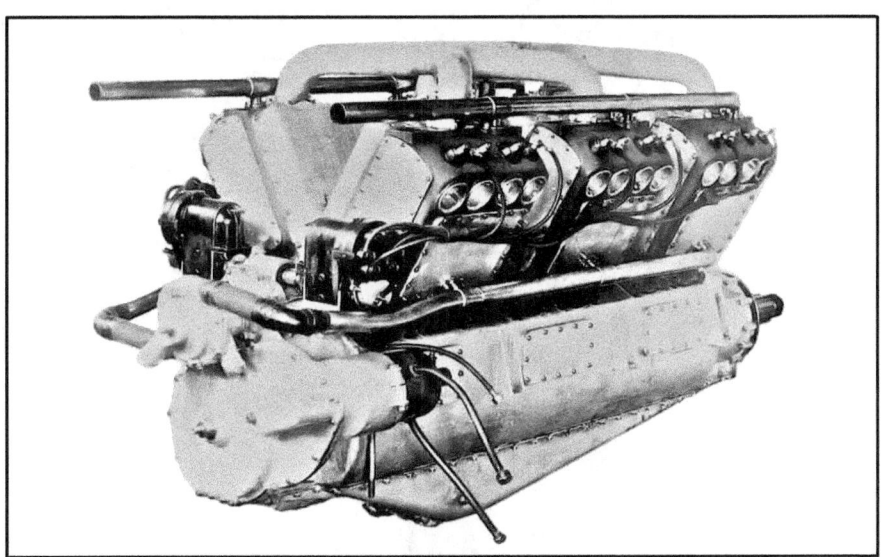

The Duesenberg V-12 with its cast cylinder pairs and separate-runner intake manifold. Visible are the plugs for valve removal and the access panels on the crankcase. The horizontal tube above each cylinder bank is the water manifold to take the coolant back to the radiator.

Completed in August of 1916, the 60° Vee engine had a bore of 4 7/8" and stroke of 7", giving a total displacement 1,568 in^3. The water-cooled engine weighed 1,040 lb including starter and generator. The engine was direct drive and generated 300 hp at 1,400 rpm and 350 hp at 1,800 rpm. It was believed that the engine could develop 400 hp at 2,100 rpm.

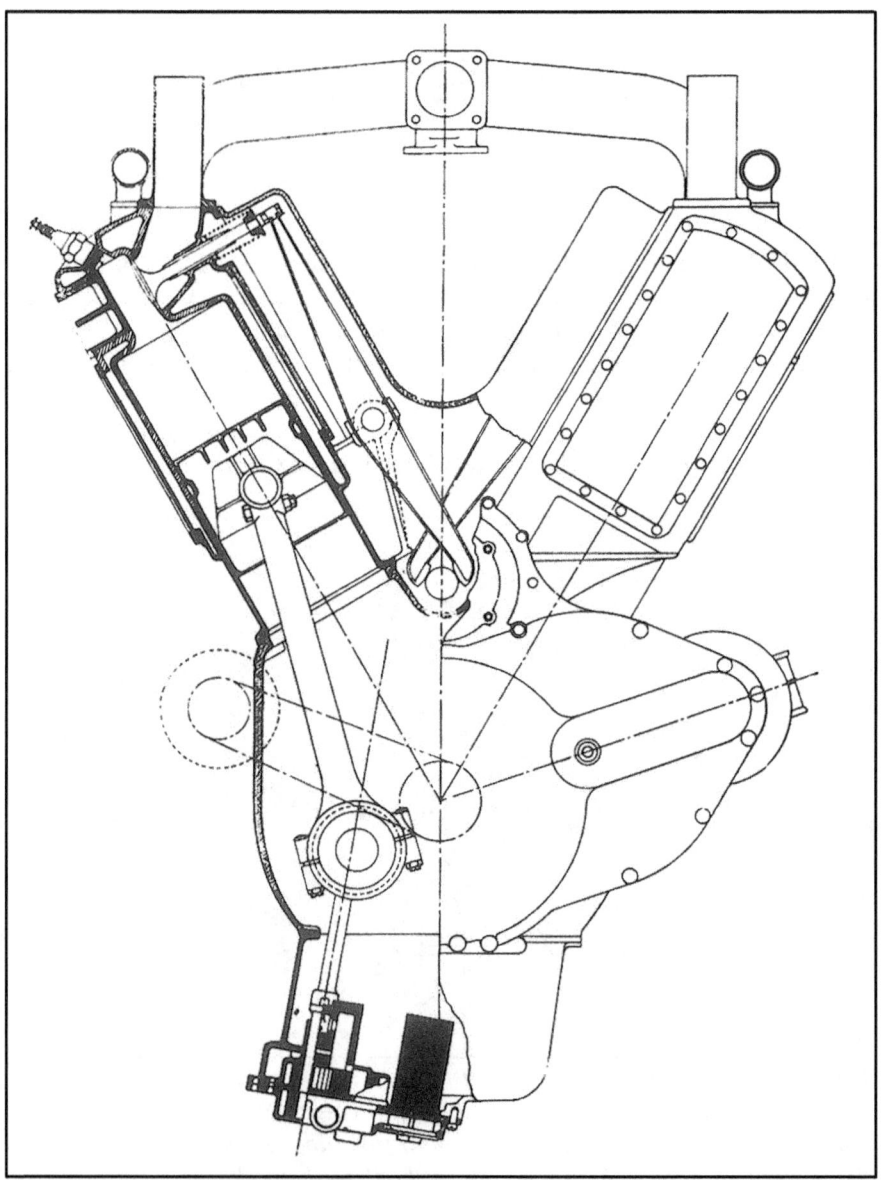

End view and sectional of the Duesenberg V-12. Of note are the large walking beam rocker arms and valve gear. The side valve and the small combustion space are clearly visible above the piston. Compare with the image on the opposite page.

4. V-12 Engine of 1916

As with the earlier four-cylinder aircraft engine, the V-12 had two side-by-side valves per cylinder and used the walking beam valve gear actuated by the camshaft, all located in the Vee of the engine. Hardened contacts were welded to the rocker arms and rode directly on the camshaft. The camshaft ran in a trough in the Vee that accumulated oil forced through the bearings. The cams dipped into this oil every revolution. The valve gear was housed in an aluminum, V-shaped cover that sat between each opposite pair of cylinders and helped stiffen the engine. As with the Special A engines, the valves could be removed through ports on the opposite side of the cylinder. These ports were sealed with threaded plugs. The two spark plugs per cylinder were now located in the head rather than in the valve access plugs, as in the earlier engine.

The cylinders were cast in pairs from semi-steel (also called grey iron, a cast iron of high quality), each pair weighing 51 lb. Three two-cylinder

Rear view of the V-12. Note the carburetors mounted to the underside of the intake manifold and the V-shaped covers for the valve gear.

pairs made up each bank of the engine. The left cylinder bank was set slightly forward of the right cylinder bank to accommodate side-by-side connecting rods. The connecting rods for each pair of opposite cylinders shared the same crankpin. The brackets supporting the valve rockers were part of the cylinder casting so that a pair of cylinders and their rockers could be removed without altering the valve adjustment.

The pistons were constructed of Magnalite aluminum, and again, were ribbed for strength and heat transfer and used a single three-piece ring. The tubular connecting rods were forged of chrome-nickel steel, first roughed out, then annealed and machined to within 1/32" of the final dimensions. They were then heat-treated, machined, and ground to the proper size. Four bolts secured the connecting rods to the crankshaft.

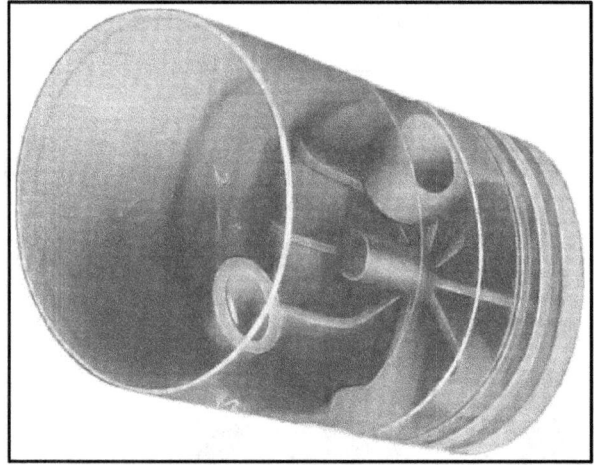

A ghost view of a Levett Magnalite piston showing the ribs leading from the piston crown to the skirt for strength and heat transfer. This is not the exact piston that was used in the V-12, but is of similar construction.

The large 3" diameter crankshaft had six throws and four main bearings. It was bored hollow, fitted with special oil tubes for the pressure lubrication system, and weighed 160 lb. The crankpins were 3" in diameter and 4 1/2" long.

The crankcase was cast from aluminum alloy and weighed 124 lb. There were three rectangular access panels along each side of the crankcase. The oil pan attached to the bottom of the crankcase and had a deep sump for oil accumulation. At the lowest point of the oil pan were two pumps. The lower scavenge pump kept the crankcase drained at all times. Oil was drawn through a strainer and delivered to an oil cooler and supply tank. The oil strainer could be removed for cleaning without disconnecting any pipes. The upper pressure pump brought in cooled oil from the tank and forced oil to all the bearings and rocker arm pivot shafts.

4. *V-12 Engine of 1916*

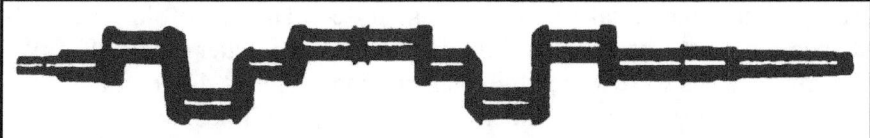

Poor quality image of the V-12's crankshaft.

Bottom view of the V-12's crankcase showing placement of the main bearings.

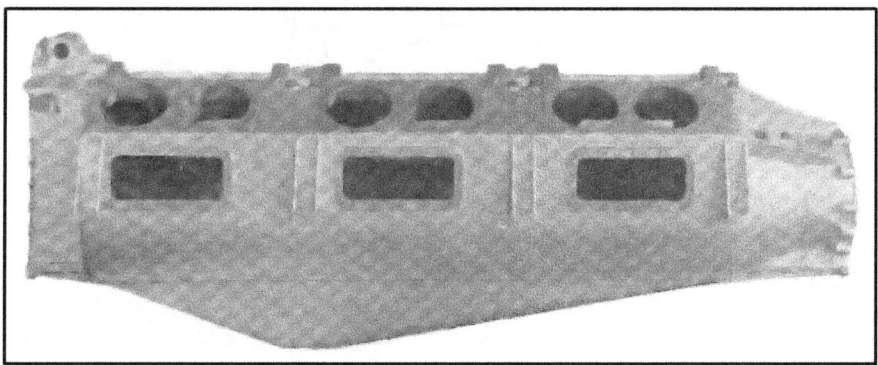

Side view of the V-12's crankcase with the oil pan attached. Note the cylinder spacing and the deep sump of the oil pan. The housing for the magneto drive is visible at the upper rear of the crankcase, and the crankcase access covers are removed.

Exhaust valves were located on the ends of each cylinder pair with the exhaust ports on top of the cylinder pair. Intake valves for the cylinder pair were located together in the middle of the pair; this enabled the cylinder pair to be fed with one intake runner. The intake manifold was located above the engine and had six separate runners that fed each cylinder pair from the top. Miller or Schebler updraft carburetors were located in the Vee between the cylinder banks and were attached to the underside of the intake manifold at its center. Either one or two carburetors could be used.

23

At least one other intake manifold was tested. This manifold was oval-shaped with straight sections directly above the cylinder banks. The two straight sections were joined by U-shaped manifolds at the front and rear. Carburetors were mounted under the U-shaped manifolds.

The V-12 engine with the oval intake manifold fitted as displayed at the Pan-American Aeronautic Exposition in 1917. A carburetor can be seen at the rear of the manifold, and another was most likely at the front. No further information has been found regarding this intake manifold.

A poor quality image of the V-12, complete with electric starter, on a test stand. Note the intake manifold is the six runner type, not the oval manifold.

4. V-12 Engine of 1916

A double centrifugal water pump was also located at the rear of the engine; it sent cooling water to each bank of three cylinder pairs through two separate outlets. The water was pumped into the bottom of aluminum plates that attached to the outside of the cylinder pair to make the water jackets. From there, it flowed up to the top of the cylinder, exited at the top of the cylinder pair through a single outlet, joined a manifold for that bank of cylinders, and then returned to the radiator. Two 12-lead Bosch magnetos provided dual ignition. The magnetos were mounted horizontally at the rear of the engine and driven by a worm gear from the camshaft. The electric starter had a gear ratio of 25 to 1. It was mounted to the timing gear cover at the rear of the engine on the right side.

The engine had a 1917 price tag of $8,500, a very large sum for the time, but it apparently never evolved past the developmental stage. Some sources say that only one test engine was built, and others cite a structural weakness that would require significant redesign to correct. At any rate, the Duesenbergs were too preoccupied with other projects to continue development of the V-12.

The V-12 ready for a run on a test stand. This appears to be the left side view of the same set-up seen on the opposite page.

An image of the Duesenberg booth at the Pan-American Aeronautic Exposition held February 8-15, 1917 in New York City. The rear of the V-12 can be seen at right under the Duesenberg sign. At left is a straight eight-cylinder marine engine.

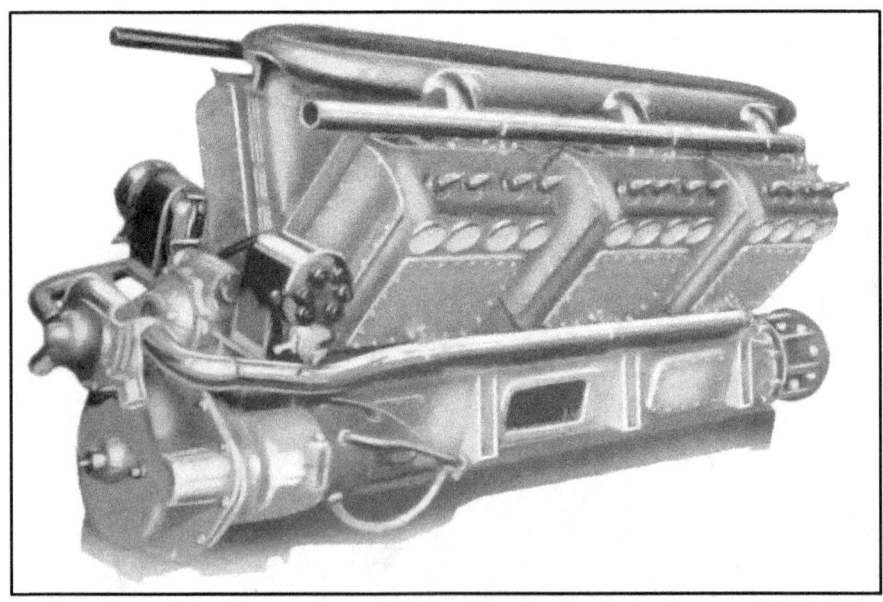

A drawing of the Duesenberg V-12 with the oval intake manifold. This appears to be a drawing of the engine as displayed at the Exposition. Compare to the image on page 24 at top.

Engine Specifications

Engine:	V-12
First Run:	1916
Type:	60° V-12, two valves per cylinder, water-cooled, aircraft engine
Horsepower:	300 hp at 1,400 rpm and 350 hp at 1,800 rpm
Displacement:	1,568 in^3
Bore:	4.875"
Stroke:	7"
BMEP:	108.2 psi at 1,400 rpm, 98.2 psi at 1,800 rpm
Specific Weight:	3.47 lb/hp at 1,400 rpm, 2.97 lb/hp at 1,800 rpm
Specific Power:	0.19 hp/in^3 at 1,400 rpm, 0.22 hp/in^3 at 1,800 rpm
Gear Reduction:	None
Carburetion:	One or two Miller or Schebler updraft
Length:	68"
Width:	31.25"
Height:	39.625"
Weight:	1,040 lb

Aircraft

M.F.P. Model D

The V-12 engine was to be used in a single engine, two-place scout biplane of standard configuration. Known as the Model D, the aircraft was designed and built by the Canadian firm M.F.P. The initials M.F.P. represented the principles of the aircraft company: Col. J. B. Miller, Walter L. Fairchild, and Walter H. Phipps. In a letter dated February 5, 1916, Fred Duesenberg indicated that his company had received a deposit from M.F.P for the engine, then under construction, with the purchase of additional units expected. However, it appears the aircraft was never built. It is not known if issues with the V-12 engine resulted in the Model D not being built or if the aircraft not being built led to the abandonment of the engine.

M.F.P. Model D Specifications (estimated)—span 38'; length 26' 10"; wing area 380 ft^2; empty weight 2,200 lb; gross weight 3,200 lb; landing speed 60 mph; max speed 130 mph.

Duesenberg wartime ad from 1918.

5. Sixteen-Valve Straight-Four Engine

An updated four-cylinder aircraft engine was created in 1916. This engine achieved a total displacement of 496 in^3 with a bore of 4 3/4" and a stroke of 7". With a gear ratio of 33 to 57, or a reduction of 0.579 to 1, the new engine had a guaranteed rating of 125 hp at 2,100 rpm but actually produced 140 hp. A direct drive version produced 100 hp at 1,400 rpm. The geared engine weighed 509 lb complete, compared to 436 lb for the direct drive version. The engine carried the 1917 price tag of $3,050 for the direct drive version and $3,500 with gear reduction.

Side view of the 16-valve, straight-four engine with the side cover removed, exposing the walking beam rocker arms for the exhaust valves. The intake valves were on the other side. Note the exhaust ports at top.

This new engine seemed to be based off of the Duesenberg four-cylinder, 16-valve auto racing engine, and again, the walking beam valve gear was used, now to actuate the four tungsten steel valves per cylinder. The left side of the engine had eight exhaust valves, while the right side had eight intake valves. The long rocker arms were operated by camshafts on either side of the aluminum, barrel type crankcase. The whole set-up was enclosed by an oil-tight, aluminum cover. The inlet valves were seated in a cage threaded into the side of the cylinder combustion chamber. This cage could be removed to allow inspection of the cylinder and the removal of the exhaust valves. The exhaust valves were seated directly in the cylinder. All valves had a throat diameter of 1 23/32" although the intake valves were 1 15/16" in diameter and exhaust valves were 2".

Aluminum plates were attached with screws at the sides and back of the monobloc cast cylinders. These plates made up the water jacket, similar to the water jacket of the V-12 engine. Water was circulated via a centrifugal pump at the rear of the engine. Coolant water entered near the bottom of the aluminum plates and was drawn upward through the jacket. There were three ports at the top of the engine through which the hot water exited into a manifold and was taken to the radiator.

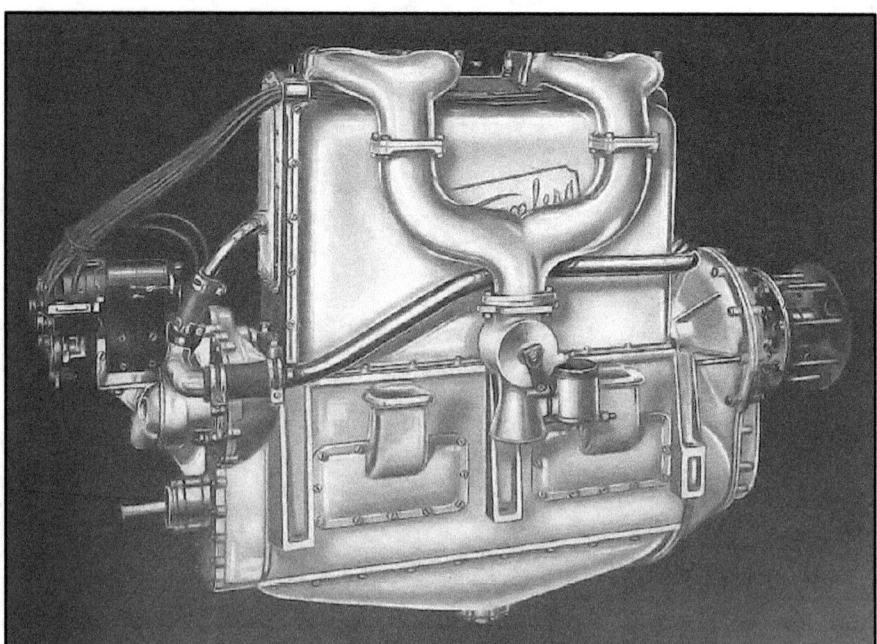

Right side of the 16-valve engine. Note the single magneto at rear and the intake manifold.

5. Sixteen-Valve Straight-Four Engine

The exhaust ports were on the left side at the top of the cylinder head. The intake was on the right side of the head and fed through a manifold that joined the first two and last two cylinders. The two intake runners traveled down the right side of the engine where they joined together and were fed by an updraft Miller carburetor. Ignition was provided by a single, eight-lead magneto that fired two spark plugs at the top of each cylinder and attached to the very end of the engine.

The hollow bore, four-throw crankshaft had three 2 1/2" diameter support bearings; the rear bearing was 4" long, and the front and middle bearings were 3 1/2" long. The chrome-nickel steel connecting rods had tubular sections, the same as the V-12 engine, with a four-bolt cap. The connecting rod bearings were 2 1/4" in diameter and 3" long. Again, a single three-piece piston ring was used on the Magnalite aluminum pistons, which were ribbed for strength and heat transfer.

The engine employed pressure lubrication of about 25 psi supplied from a pump submerged in the detachable oil pan. Oil flowed through cored passageways in the crankshaft to the three main bearings and through tubes located under each connecting rod. These tubes created a spray of oil that

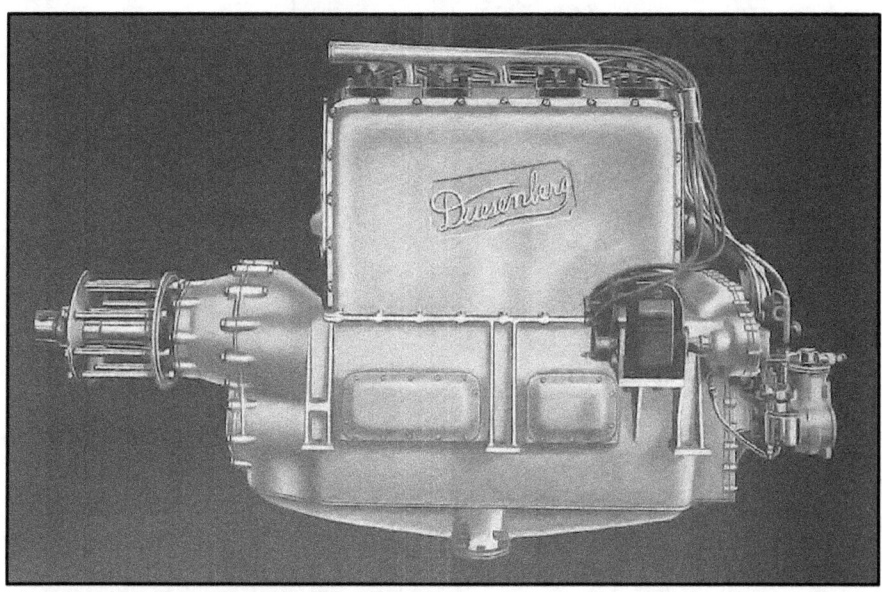

Updated engine of late 1917. Compare to the image on the opposite page. Note the updated gear reduction housing, the two magnetos now located one on each side, the updated rear housing for the magneto drive, and the Christensen self-starter at the extreme rear. The tubular manifold above the engine was the exit for the coolant water.

the connecting rod and crankpin would pass through. The oil was then thrown from the rod and lubricated the rest of the engine. In addition, a splash system accumulated oil in a trough under each connecting rod. These troughs were constructed so that no matter the angle of the engine, oil was retained in the trough. The oil returned by gravity to the pan where it was strained. Oil was also pressure fed to the rocker arm pivot shaft, but the valves used splash lubrication. On both sides of the crankcase were two rectangular access plates with breathers incorporated on the right side.

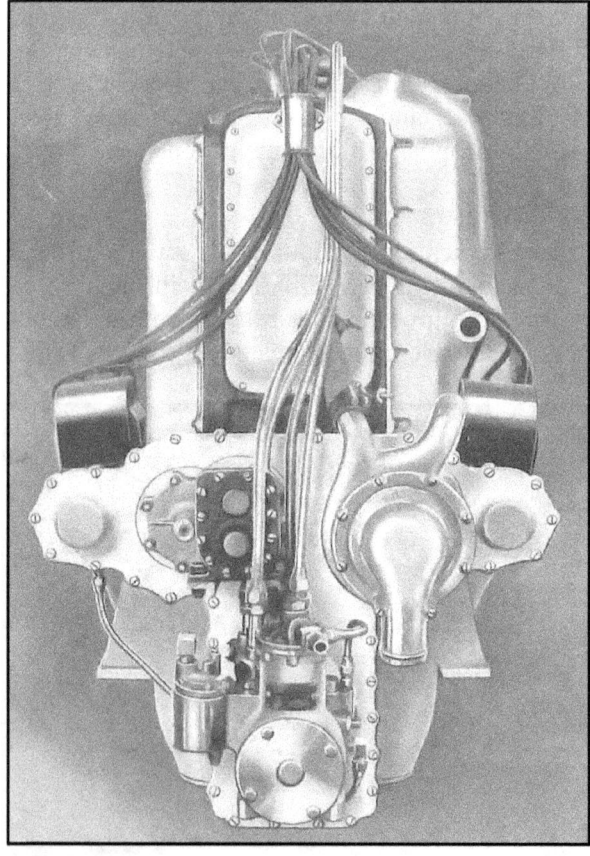

Rear view of the updated 1917 engine showing the dual magnetos to advantage. The Christensen self-starter is at the very bottom of the image.

The engine was equipped with a Christensen self-starter (see Appendix E). Designed by Niels A. Christensen, the starter drew in pressurized air from a storage tank. The compressed air was mixed with fuel in the starter unit, and the mixture was then fed to the engine cylinders in successive firing order. The charge of fuel and air filled the cylinder, acting as the compression stroke. This charge forced the piston down and was subsequently ignited by the spark plug, achieving the power stroke and starting the engine. The starter was attached to the rear of the engine at the crankshaft. As the engine was turned over by the starter, the crankshaft actuated the starter's valves that fed the air and fuel mixture to the next cylinder in firing order.

Late in 1917, the engine was updated and lightened. The changes were mostly external, with the engine maintaining the same bore, stroke, and power. Two Bosch magnetos, one on each side, were now mounted toward the rear of the engine. This change necessitated a new casting to encase the horizontal drive for the magnetos. In addition, the crankcase casting was updated with mounts for the magnetos and a smaller rear access panel on the crankcase sides to accommodate these updated mounts. The gear reduction housing was also updated. The engine's weight decreased 39 lb for the geared version and 9 lb for the direct drive version, resulting in engine weights of 470 lb and 425 lb, respectively.

Engine Specifications

Engine:	4-cylinder, 16-valve
First Run:	1916
Type:	Straight 4-cylinder, four valves per cylinder, water-cooled, aircraft engine
Horsepower:	Direct 100 hp at 1,500,
	Geared 125 hp at 2,100 rpm (rated) but produced 140 hp
Displacement:	496 in^3
Bore:	4.75"
Stroke:	7"
BMEP:	Direct 106.5 psi,
	Geared 95.0 psi (106.5 psi at 140 hp)
Specific Weight:	Direct 4.36 lb/hp,
	Geared 4.07 lb/hp (3.64 lb/hp at 140 hp)
	Late 1917: Direct 4.25 lb/hp,
	Geared 3.76 lb/hp (3.36 lb/hp at 140 hp)
Specific Power:	Direct 0.20 hp/in^3
	Geared 0.25 hp/in^3 (0.28 hp/in^3 at 140 hp)
Gear Reduction:	None or 0.579:1
Carburetion:	One Miller updraft
Length:	43.375"
Width:	15.5"
Height:	37.5"
Weight:	Direct 436 lb, Geared 509 lb
	Late 1917: Direct 425 lb, Geared 470 lb

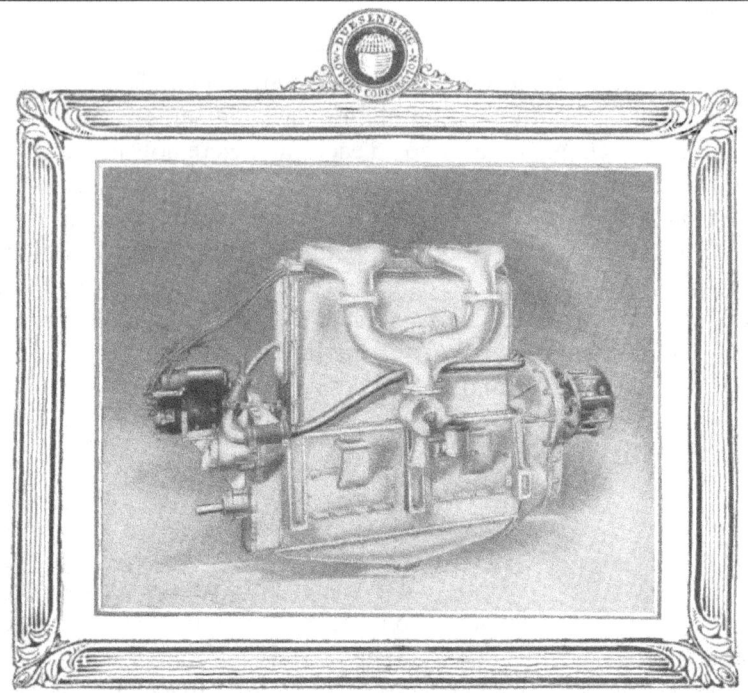

Duesenberg ad for the 16-valve, straight four-cylinder from 1917.

5. Sixteen-Valve Straight-Four Engine

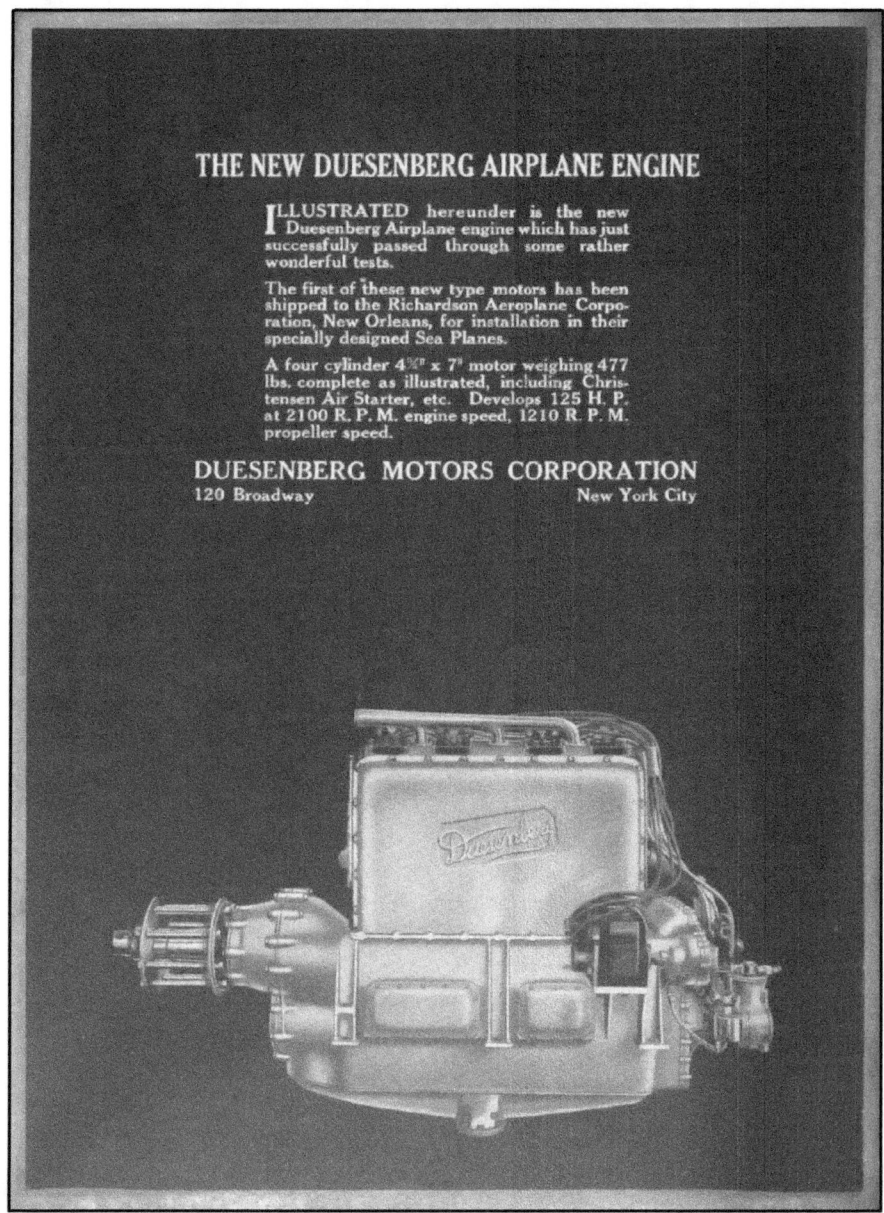

Duesenberg ad from November 1917 with the updated four-cylinder engine pictured. The ad also states the engine was to be used in the Richardson Aeroplane Corporation's flying boat, but no proof has been found that it was.

Aircraft

Gallaudet D-1
Reportedly, two special engines of 150 hp were used in the Gallaudet D-1, which was given the Navy serial number AH-61 (later A59). This was most likely the first aircraft to be powered by Duesenberg engines. Edson Gallaudet, the aircraft's designer, traveled to the Duesenberg plant on February 11, 1916 to supervise the final work on the engines. The first engine had been tested and shipped to the Gallaudet plant by the end of February, and the second engine followed in mid-March 1916.

The Gallaudet D-1 was a large, two-place biplane pusher fitted with a single large float beneath the fuselage and two smaller wing tip floats. What was truly unique about the aircraft was the "Gallaudet Drive" system of propulsion (U.S. patent 1,262,660). The two Duesenberg engines were mounted side-by-side in the fuselage, aft of the cockpit but forward of a four-blade propeller that was mounted in the center of the fuselage between the wings and tail. The propeller hub was enclosed by a metal ring the same diameter as the fuselage, with just the propeller blades protruding from the ring. This ring ran on ball bearing races surrounding a fixed steel drum that was the main structural member supporting the aft fuselage and tail. Either one or both of the engines could drive the propeller through flexible couplings and with spur reduction gears that meshed with a large gear attached to the propeller ring.

The D-1 was first flown on July 17, 1916 by David McCullach. Some trouble was experienced with the Duesenberg engines during testing. On one flight in October 1916, a small break occurred in the head of the number one piston of the port engine. Duesenberg mechanics installed newly designed pistons and gave the engines a general overhaul. However, trouble was also encountered with engine overheating and preignition caused by poor water circulation. The engines were put on a test stand where more troubleshooting was done and were reinstalled in the D-1 by late November 1916. A bit more trouble was encountered with the engines backfiring. The magnetos were given a thorough cleaning that resolved the problem. With the engines now working reliably, official Navy trials were conducted in late January 1917, and no engine trouble was encountered. Late in 1917, the updated, lighter version of the 16-valve engine replaced the original engines installed in the D-1, but by that time the Navy had apparently lost interest in the aircraft. In early 1918, one of the D-1's engines was removed and shipped to the Bureau of Steam Engineering in New York City where it was used for instructional purposes. Only one Gallaudet D-1 aircraft was built.

Some sources say the follow-on D-2 was also powered by the Duesenberg four-cylinder, but it was actually powered by two 150 hp Hall-Scott A-5a engines.

The Gallaudet D-1 with its twin Duesenberg engines that powered the pusher propeller mounted in the fuselage.

Another view of the unique two-place Gallaudet D-1 pusher.

Gallaudet D-1 Specifications—span 48'; length 33'; wing area 656 ft^2; empty weight 3,600 lb; gross weight 4,604 lb; range 288 mi; climb to 5,000' 5 min 32 sec; landing speed 60 mph; max speed 90 mph.

Orenco Type A
A direct drive version of this engine was used in a two-place primary trainer biplane of conventional layout known as the Orenco Type A (Ordnance Engineering Corporation Type A). The trainer had side-by-side seating with dual-controls for the instructor and trainee. The Orenco Type A first flew on February 24, 1917 piloted by Bert Acosta. Two examples were built.

Orenco Type A Specifications—span 44'; length 26' 7"; height 10' 6"; wing area 430 ft^2; empty weight 1,476 lb; gross weight 2,167 lb; range 306 mi; climb to 5,000'; 15 min 0 sec; landing speed 38 mph, max speed 74 mph.

The Orenco Type A trainer. Note the front wheel to prevent nose overs.

Lanzius L1
A geared version of this engine was used in the Lanzius L1 biplane trainer. The aircraft was a two-place biplane of conventional layout, with the exception of a variable incidence wing.

Designed by George Lanzius, each wing of the Lanzius L1 pivoted around its main spar to change the angle of incidence (U.S. patent 1,289,206). Together, the wings could be varied from 0° to 15° by the pilot while in flight. This design used an external horizontal truss above the upper and below the lower wings. While the variable incidence wings had the advantage of lowering the plane's landing speed, the trusses increased drag considerably.

5. Sixteen-Valve Straight-Four Engine

Piloted by Canadian Erroll Boyd, the L1's first and only flight occurred on July 1, 1917. Boyd lost lateral control during the flight and the aircraft crashed. Boyd was thrown free from the crash and escaped unharmed, but the sole Lanzius L1 was destroyed.

Two further designs came from Lanzius: the LII and the Speed Scout. Contrary to what some sources claim, neither was powered by a Duesenberg engine.

Lanzius L1 Specifications—span 38'; length 25'; empty weight 1,300 lb; gross weight 2,100 lb.

Lanzius L1 with its variable incidence wings and gear drive Duesenberg engine. Note the counter-clockwise rotation of the propeller. Because spur reduction gears were used, it appears the propeller rotated counter-clockwise on the engine with gear reduction and clockwise on the engine with direct drive.

Unconfirmed Aircraft

In 1916, one version of the Lawrence-Lewis A model flying boat and, in 1917, the Richardson Aeroplane Corporation's flying boat were both reported to use or have planned to use the geared version of the 16-valve, four-cylinder engine. No further information has been found that supports Duesenberg engines actually being used. Many sources cite other engines being flown in these aircraft, with no mention of Duesenberg engines. Neither aircraft entered production, and whether they were ever flown with Duesenberg power has been lost to history for now.

Duesenberg ad from 1917 featuring the Ordinance Engineering Corporation (Orenco) trainer.

5. Sixteen-Valve Straight-Four Engine

Lanzius ad from 1917 featuring the L1 and the Duesenberg engine. Note the external truss above the upper wing and below the lower wing.

Duesenberg ad from 1917 featuring what appears to be the Lanzius L1. Note the external trusses on the wings and the exhaust manifold extending above the engine. Compare to the images of the Lanzius L1 on pages 39 and 41.

6. The King-Bugatti U-16 Engine

On November 20, 1917, Duesenberg Motors Corporation was contracted to produce 500 Liberty V-12 engines. This number was doubled on December 11, 1917. Duesenberg had already begun to equip its plant for production of the Liberty engine when the order was changed to the Bugatti U-16 engine on January 4, 1918. Ultimately, Duesenberg would be contracted for 2,000 Bugatti engines, plus spares.

The King-Bugatti U-16 engine produced by Duesenberg.

The Bugatti engine was essentially two straight-eight engines side-by-side on a common aluminum crankcase. The two crankshafts were geared to a common hollow propeller shaft through which a 37mm cannon barrel could be fitted. Each crankshaft was made of two pieces joined in the center. The front end of the rear half was tapered with a key and was inserted into the rear end of the front half. The two halves were then drawn together with a nut. Each section of the shaft formed a four-cylinder crankshaft with the throws all in one plane. The throws of the two sections of the shaft were at right angles.

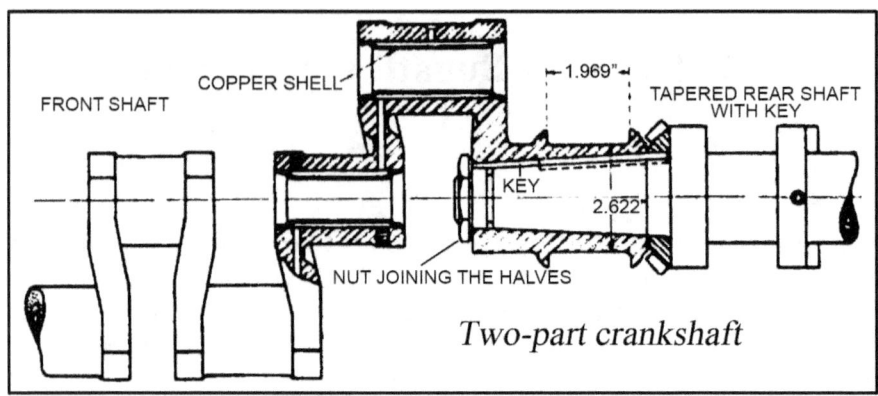

Connection of the two crankshaft halves.

Each eight-cylinder bank was made up of two cast iron, four-cylinder blocks. Each cylinder had two vertical inlet valves and a single vertical exhaust valve all actuated by rockers that were operated from the single overhead camshaft. The camshaft was driven by a vertical shaft positioned between the two four-cylinder blocks. Each of the four carburetors fed four cylinders via a water jacketed manifold. Each cylinder exhausted into an individual stack in the space between the cylinder blocks.

Ettore Bugatti had built the prototype U-16 engine in France in 1915. In 1917, he presented this engine to the Bolling Commission, which was sent to Europe from the United States to acquire European military aeronautical technology that could be built in the United States. During testing in Paris, an American soldier walked in front of the running engine; he was stuck by the propeller and killed, becoming the first active duty U.S. casualty of World War I. With only 37 hours of testing, the Bugatti U-16 prototype was sent to the U.S. for manufacture. The engine was tested at McCook Field in Dayton, Ohio and then sent to the Duesenberg plant. Charles Brady King of the Signal Corps was sent to test and rework the engine as needed. During a run in February 1918, the prototype U-16 engine blew apart because of a structural weakness.

As a result, King incorporated many changes and improvements, and the engine was now known as the King-Bugatti. The splash lubrication was replaced with a pressure system, and general improvements were made to the oil circulation. The cylinder water jackets were updated, and water circulation was improved. The water pump was modified to prevent leakage of coolant water into the crankcase. The propeller reduction gears were modified, resulting in a ratio change from 0.681:1 to 0.667:1, and the propeller was moved 3 3/4" forward. The thrust and crankshaft bearings were redesigned and improved. Some general changes were made to the connecting rods, and liners were added to the rod ends. The King-Bugatti's pistons were redesigned and the number of piston rings reduced to three from the original five. The intake and exhaust valve seats were thickened to prevent cracks from forming in the head. The rocker arms were redesigned to ease manufacture. Each of the original engine's rocker arms required 14 machining operations, while the King-Bugatti's required only four. The original engine required 672 machine operations to produce its

An early King-Bugatti engine. Note the differences in the gear reduction case and the intake manifolds from the King-Bugatti image on page 43.

its 48 rocker arms, while the King-Bugatti required only 192. The front carburetors on each side of the engine were relocated to make fuel distribution more uniform. The original engine used four magnetos, but the King-Bugatti engine used only two. This change alone reduced the engine's weight by 40 pounds.

The end result of all these changes was an engine that was easier to manufacture, lighter, more powerful, and more reliable. Delays with manufacturing the engine (and the crankshaft in particular) resulted in the first engine that met production specifications being run in July 1918. However, fuel and oil consumption were high.

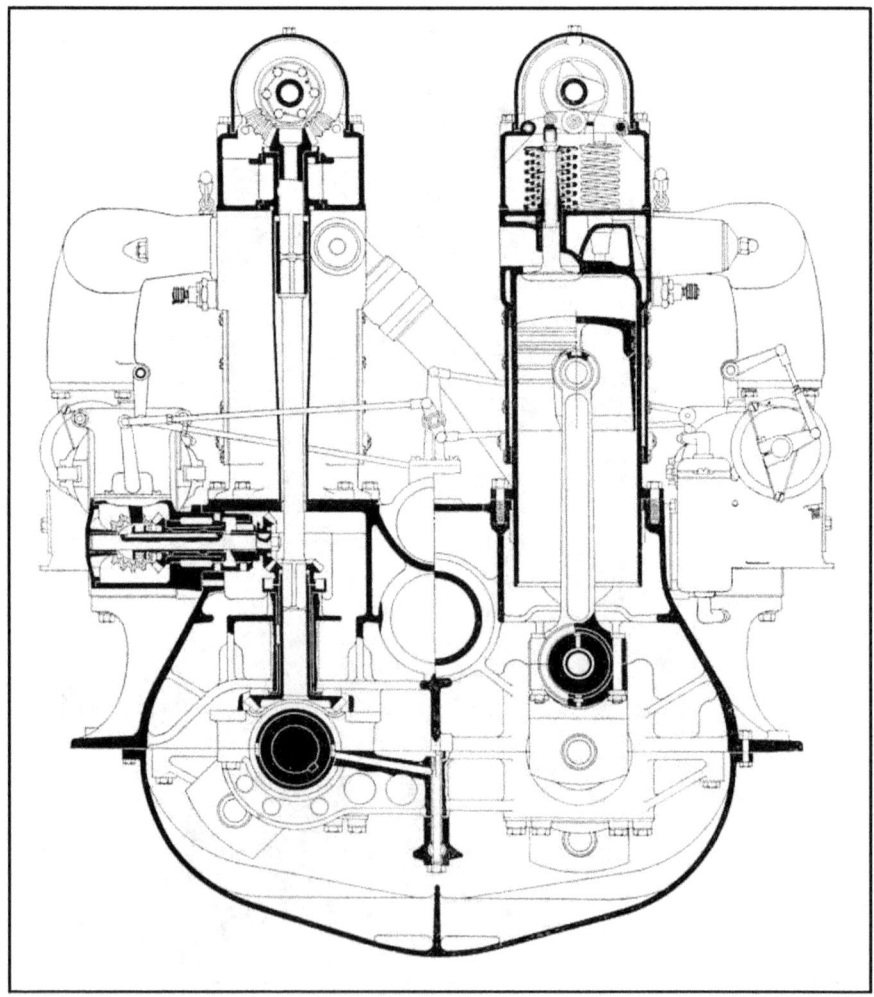

Sectional end view of the King-Bugatti.

To fix the problems and get the engine into production, nine test engines ran 110 hours from July to September 1918. The problems were overcome, and the King-Bugatti passed its 50 hour type test at the Duesenberg engine test house in October 1918.

The King-Bugatti displaced 1,484 in^3 from the 16 cylinders of 4.33" bore and 6.3" stroke. The engine weighed 1,248 lb dry and another 38 lb with water in the jackets, for a total of 1,286 lb. At 2,000 rpm, it produced 410 hp at the propeller. On a dynamometer in August of 1918, A King-Bugatti test engine achieved a power reading of 500 hp at 2,300 rpm but with significant wear and tear on the test engine.

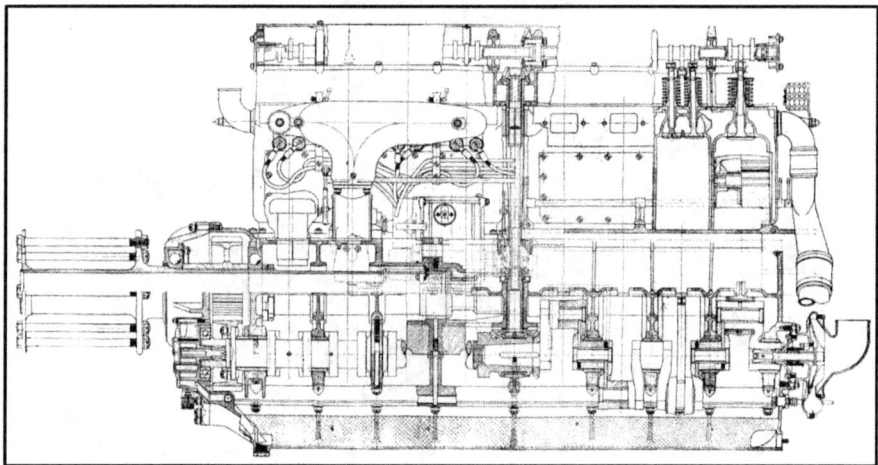

King-Bugatti sectional side view above and top view below.

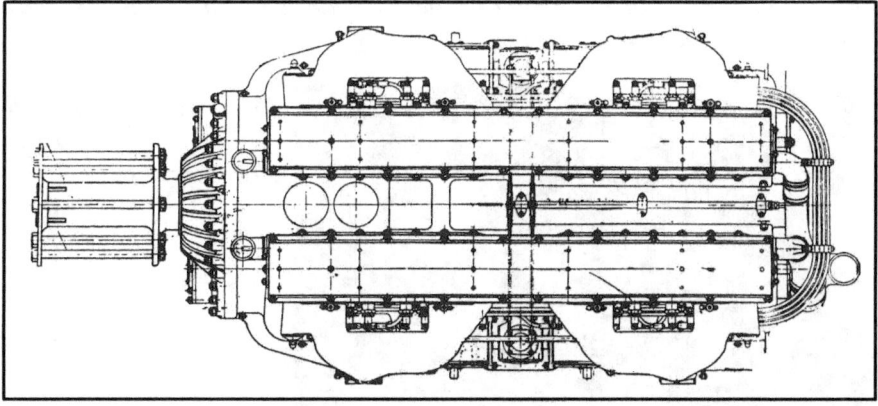

By early November 1918, 11 King-Bugatti production engines had been delivered: six engines were sent to Packard for installation in Packard-LePère aircraft that were under construction; four engines went to the Air

Service; one engine went to McCook Field. Although Duesenberg was contracted for 2,000 King-Bugatti engines, only 40 were officially tested and accepted by the Army. The remaining engines were immediately cancelled after the Armistice on November 11, 1918. However, Duesenberg continued to assemble the engines into January 1919, with perhaps 60 being made.

A King-Bugatti engine under test in the Duesenberg engine test house. The man under the Y-shaped coolant header is Charles B. King (Bugatti Trust photo, www.bugatti-trust.co.uk).

A smartly dressed Duesenberg worker transporting 24 King-Bugatti crankshaft halves, enough for six engines.

6. The King-Bugatti U-16 Engine

Duesenberg workers machining crankshafts for the King-Bugatti.

With its problems mostly worked out, the King-Bugatti engine could have stayed in production had it not been for the Liberty V-12 engine. The Liberty produced about the same power, but the Liberty was lighter, cheaper, more reliable, and already in full production, with over 20,000 built. The Liberty, combined with the war's end, meant no future for the King-Bugatti. A few King-Bugatti engines were sold as surplus, including two that powered A. L. Judson's *Whip-Po'-Will Jr.* race boat.

About 25 complete King-Bugatti engines lined up at the Duesenberg plant.

49

Engine Specifications

Engine:	King-Bugatti U-16
First Run:	1918 (1915 for the Bugatti prototype)
Type:	U-16, three valves per cylinder, water-cooled, aircraft engine
Horsepower:	410 hp at 2,000 rpm
Displacement:	1,484 in^3
Bore:	4.33" (110 mm)
Stroke:	6.3" (160 mm)
Compression Ratio:	5:1
BMEP:	109.4 psi
Specific Weight:	3.04 lb/hp
Specific Power:	0.28 hp/in^3
Gear Reduction:	0.667:1 (0.681:1 for the Bugatti prototype)
Carburetion:	Four Miller updraft
Firing order:	1L, 7R, 5L, 4R, 3L, 8R, 7L, 2R, 4L, 6R, 8L, 1R, 2L, 5R, 6L, 3R
Length:	44.25" (1,124 mm)
Width:	24.80" (630 mm)
Height:	32.28" (820 mm)
Weight:	1,248 lb (566 kg)

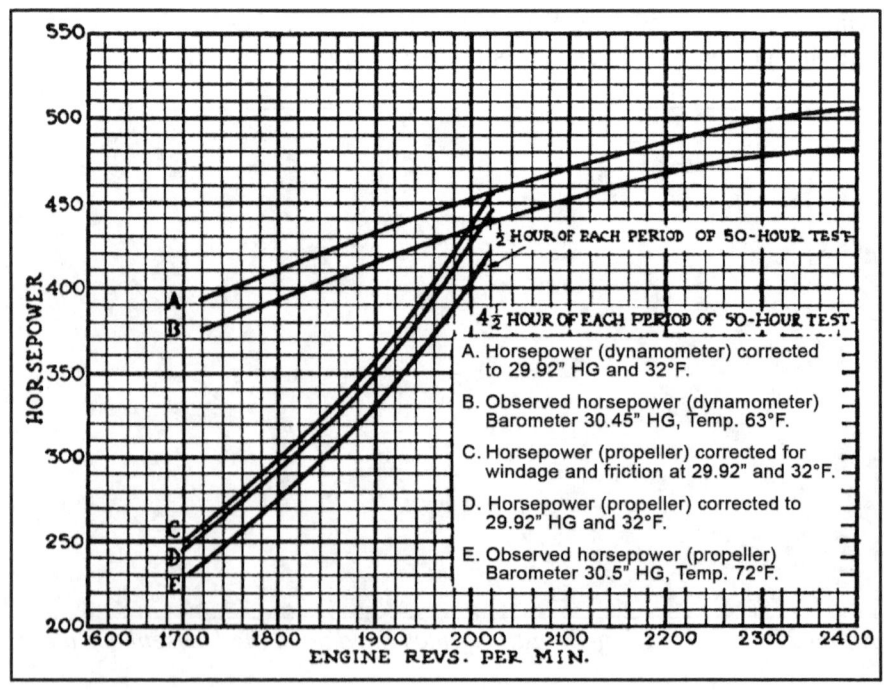

Survivors

At least four King-Bugatti engines have survived, three of them complete. One complete engine can be seen in the Auburn-Cord-Duesenberg Museum in Auburn, Indiana; another at the National Museum of the United States Air Force at Wright-Patterson Air Force Base in Dayton, Ohio; and the third at the National Air Museum Steven F. Udvar-Hazy Center in Chantilly, Virginia. The Bugatti Trust in Gotherington, Gloucestershire, UK has an incomplete cutaway King-Bugatti engine which, of course, they refer to as the Bugatti-King—perhaps rightly so.

Front view of the King-Bugatti engine in the Auburn-Cord-Duesenberg Museum in Auburn, Indiana (Perfesser photo via the Wikimedia Commons).

Above and Below—The King Bugatti on display at the National Museum of the United States Air Force at Wright-Patterson Air Force Base in Dayton, Ohio. Note the exhaust stacks between the cylinder banks (Photos © Gary Brossett 2004, via the Aircraft Engine Historical Society, www.enginehistory.com).

6. The King-Bugatti U-16 Engine

Above—King-Bugatti on display at the National Air Museum Steven F. Udvar-Hazy Center in Chantilly, Virginia (Kogo photo via the Wikimedia Commons). Below—The partially assembled, cutaway "Bugatti-King" engine at the Bugatti Trust in Gotherington, Gloucestershire, UK. Completed in 2010, the Bugatti Trust had a replica crankcase built for this engine (Bugatti Trust photo, www.bugatti-trust.co.uk).

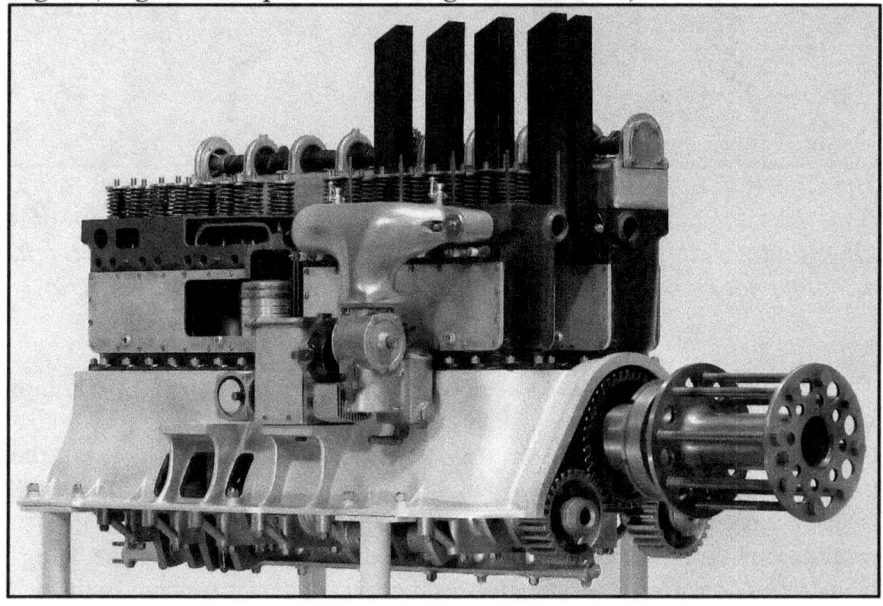

Aircraft

Packard-LePère LUSAC-21

The King-Bugatti engine was installed in three LUSAC-21 airframes. While the first aircraft flew in November 1918, it is doubtful the others were ever flown. Designed by Georges LePère and built by Packard in Detroit, Michigan late in 1918, the LUSAC-21 (LePère United States Army Combat-21) was a tandem, two-seat biplane fighter of normal tractor configuration. Others of the type were built, but they were powered by the Liberty engine and known as the LUSAC-11. The Liberty-powered LUSAC-11 was about two feet shorter and a couple hundred pounds lighter than the King-Bugatti-powered LUSAC-21. In addition, the LUSAC-21 used a four-blade propeller.

Packard-LePère LUSAC-21 Specifications—span 41' 7"; length 27' 1"; height 10' 7"; wing area 416 ft^2; gross weight 4,485 lb; landing speed 50 mph; max speed 120 mph.

The LUSAC-21: perhaps the only King-Bugatti-powered aircraft to fly. Note the vertical exhaust stack in front of the upper wing. The nose of a Liberty-powered LUSAC-11 can be seen in the background at left. Although not apparent in this image, the two aircraft were very similar.

Packard-LePère LUSAGH-11

The King-Bugatti was also intended to power the LUSAGH-11 (LePère United States Army Ground Harassment-11), which was a two-seat biplane of normal construction. It was similar to the LUSAC-21, but the pilot and gunner sat side-by-side in an armored cockpit. Originally, three aircraft were ordered, but one was converted to Liberty power due to production issues with the King-Bugatti engine. Apparently, the King-Bugatti version was not completed, and the last aircraft was not built.

Packard-LePère LUSAGH-11 Specifications—span 47' 1"; length 26'; height 10' 10"; wing area 601 ft^2; empty weight 4,100 lb; gross weight 5,620 lb; range 278 mi; landing speed 61 mph; max speed 117 mph.

The King-Bugatti-powered LUSAGH-11 under construction at the Packard factory in Detroit, Michigan at the end of August 1918. Note the exhaust manifold combining the 16 individual exhaust stacks into one vertical pipe and the radiator below the propeller shaft. This aircraft was never completed.

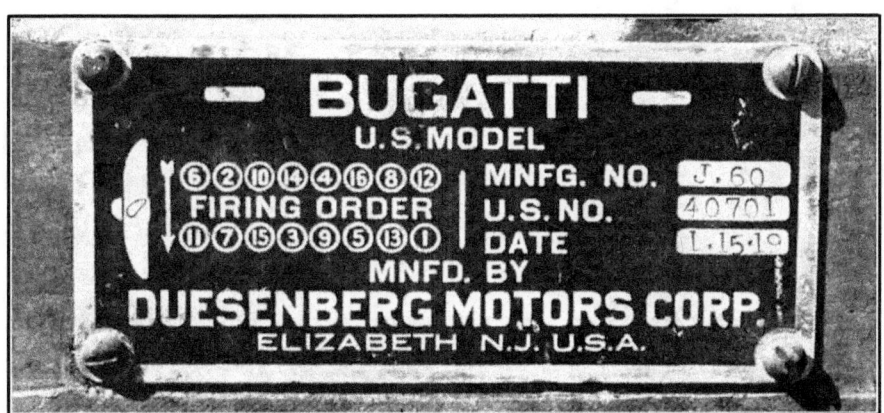

The data plate on a King-Bugatti engine baring the manufacturing number J.60 and indicating it was built on January 15, 1919, over two months after the Duesenberg/King-Bugatti contract was cancelled by the U.S. government.

Duesenberg airplane engine ad from 1917 with a stylized Lanzius L1 aircraft. Note the external trusses on the wings.

7. Duesenberg Model H V-16 Engine

Early in WWI, J. R. Harbeck, President of the Duesenberg Motors Corporation, suggested a plan to design and build an 800 hp aircraft engine. This engine was larger and more powerful than anything being produced. The U.S. government awarded a contract to the Duesenberg Motors Corporation to develop this aircraft engine. The original contract placed in April 1918 was for two geared engines, but this contract was changed in June to one geared drive engine and one direct drive engine. The order was later expanded to include two engines of each type, with one pair going to the Army and the other pair to the Navy.

Duesenberg Model H engine with gear reduction. Note the plugs for valve removal on each cylinder and the many crankcase breathers that were only on the right side of the engine. The crankcase was partitioned into four sections by the air passageways that ran through the crankcase and fed the carburetors. Each section needed its own breathers.

Fred Duesenberg, with the assistance of William Beckman, Cornelius W. Van Ranst, and George Dennis, spent much of 1918 on the design of the engine, now known as the Model H. While the Model H was designed at the same time the Bugatti U-16 was being worked on, the Model H had nothing in common with the Bugatti. However, many of the Model H's features did come from the 16-valve, four-cylinder aircraft engine of 1916 and other Duesenberg designs. The first prototype, a geared drive engine, was completed in June 1918, with the direct drive engine following in

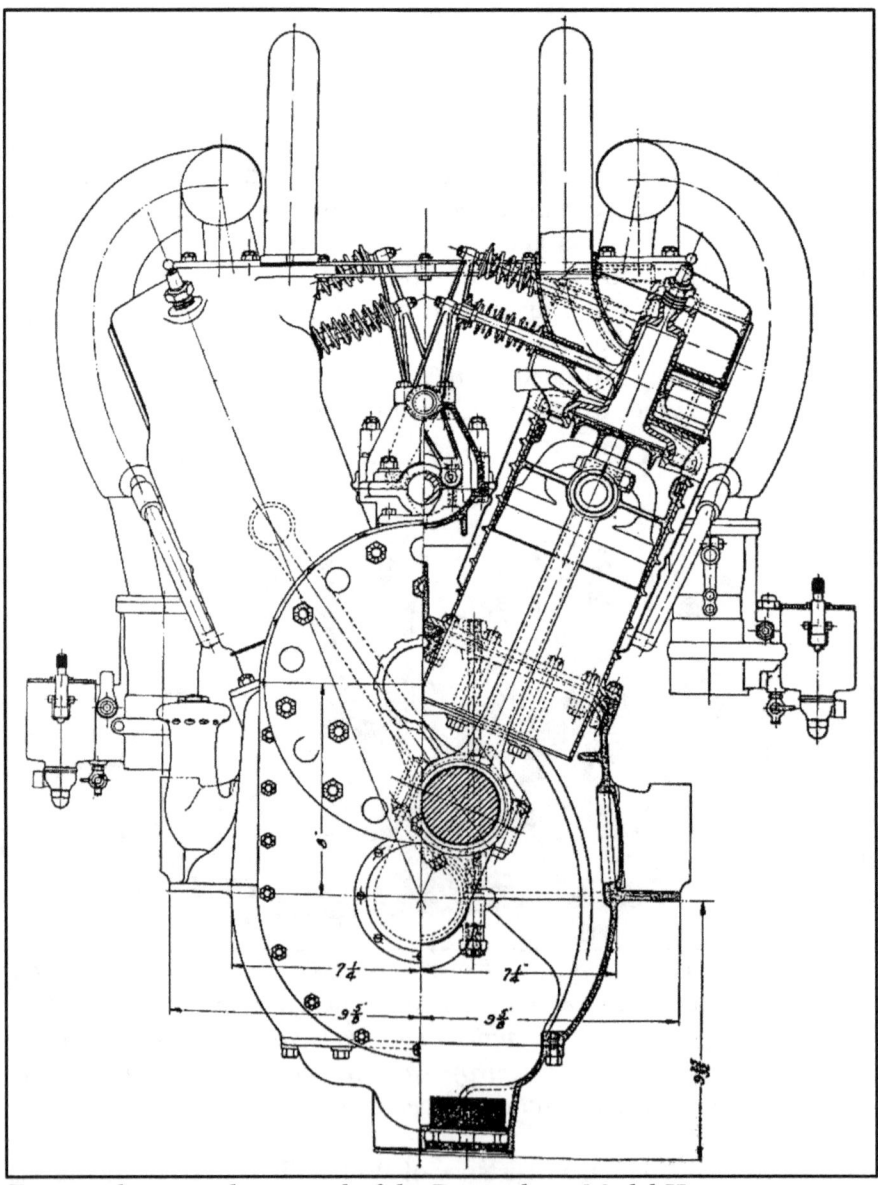

Front end view and sectional of the Duesenberg Model H.

January of 1919. After the first engine, subsequent engines incorporated some slight design changes suggested by manufacturing and tests of the first engine.

The Model H was a 45° V-16 aircraft engine. The geared drive version (H-1) produced 800 hp at 1,800 rpm, and the direct drive version (H-2) produced 700 hp at 1,550 rpm. The water-cooled engine had individual cylinders, a first for Duesenberg, constructed in the fashion pioneered by Mercedes. The Model H was an undersquare engine with a bore of 6" and

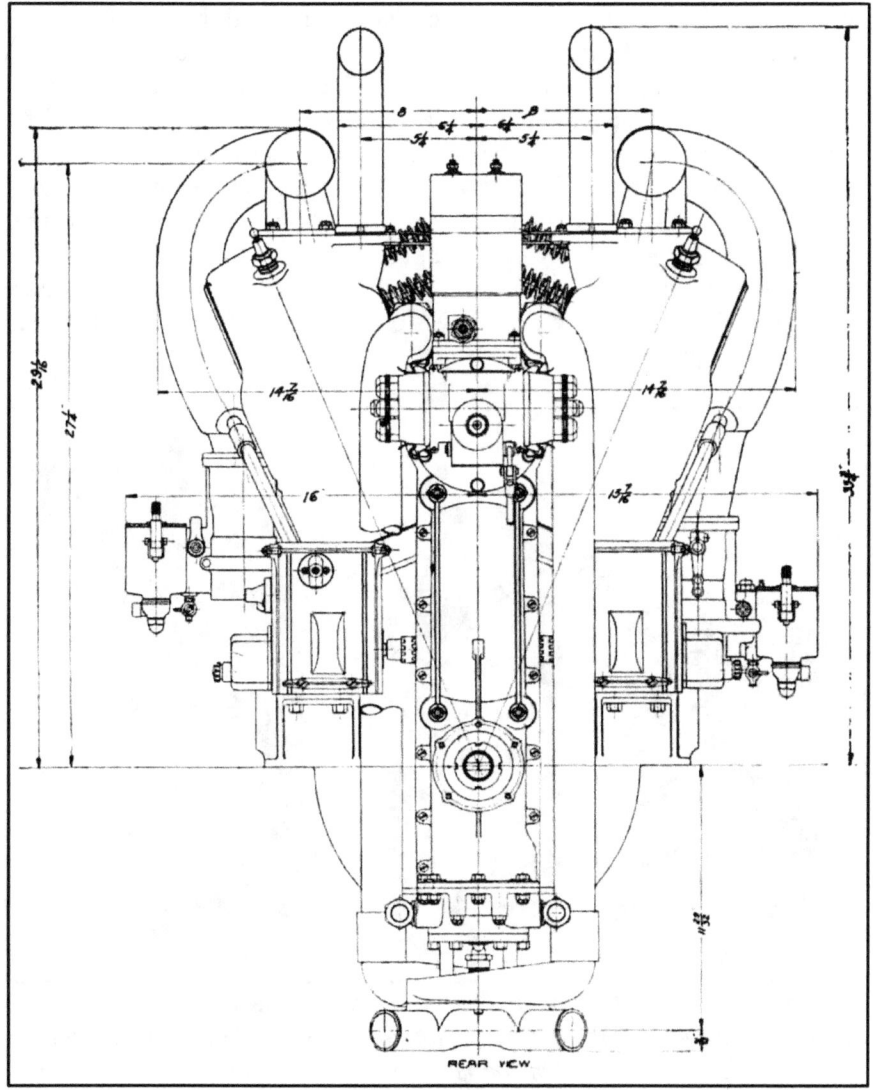

Rear end view of the Duesenberg Model H.

a stroke of 7 1/2", giving a total displacement of 3,393 in^3. The engine's compression ratio was about 4.66 to 1. The geared version weighed 1,575 lb and the direct drive version weighed 1,390 lb.

The gear reduction was the plain spur type, having a 25 to 33 ratio (0.758 reduction). At an engine speed of 1,800 rpm, the propeller speed was 1,360 rpm. The reduction gears were 3 5/8" wide with a 4" face. The propeller rotated counter-clockwise because of the spur gears. The reduction gear housing was cast integral with the aluminum crankcase, but the gear bearings were located in steel plates secured to the housing by numerous bolts. These very strong steel bearing plates prevented the bearings from spreading in spite of the enormous radial pressure created by the gears. The direct drive engine used a different crankcase casting than the geared drive engine. The crankcase tapered down at the front of the crankshaft to support the thrust bearing and the propeller hub. There were no provisions for gear reduction on the direct drive engine casting, and there would have been no way to alter the crankcase to incorporate gear reduction. Because the propeller for the direct drive engine was mounted directly on the crankshaft, it was 8" lower than on the geared engine and rotated clockwise. The direct drive engine was only slightly, if at all, shorter than the geared engine.

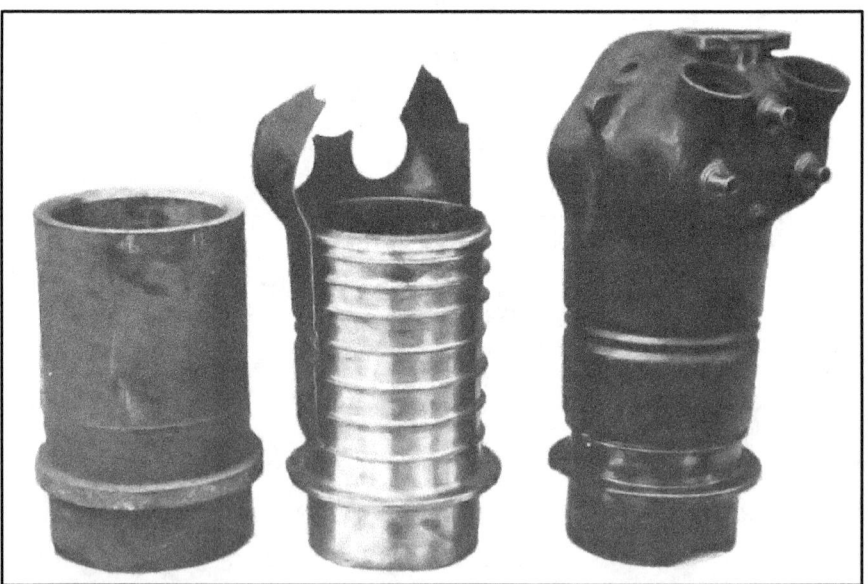

Duesenberg Model H cylinder. On the left is the raw cylinder forging. In the middle is the machined barrel; note the ribs. Half of the water jacket is attached to the barrel. On the right is the complete cylinder. Note the corrugations in the middle of the completed cylinder's water jacket.

The cylinder barrels were made individually and constructed of chrome-nickel steel forgings open at both ends. The barrel was case hardened on the inside to afford the best track for the aluminum piston. The cylinder barrel had seven strengthening ribs running parallel around the outer circumference. The ribs not only strengthened the barrel, they also helped dissipate the heat from the cylinder to the cooling water. The barrel was tapered, but average wall thickness was 1/8". A 1/4" base flange attached the cylinder to the aluminum crankcase via nine studs, and the cylinder extended 2 3/4" into the crankcase.

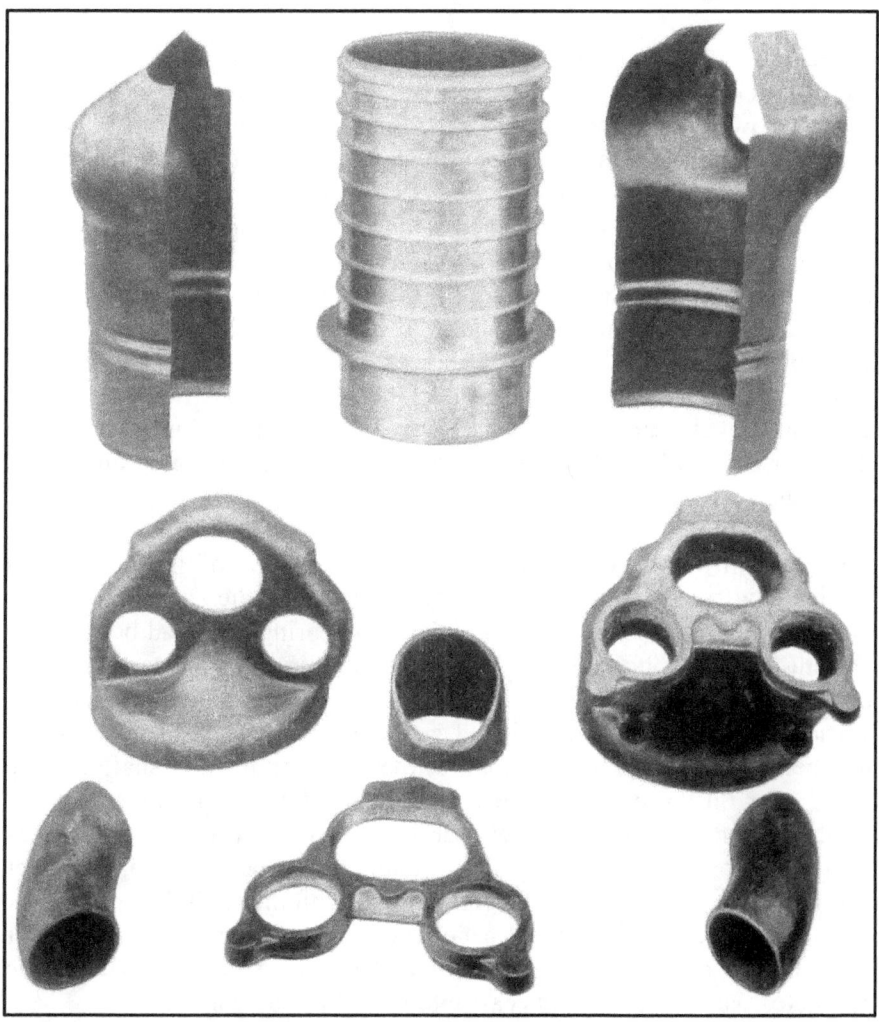

The steel stampings of the water jacket with the finished cylinder barrel in between, and the steel stampings that made up the cylinder head.

The cylinder heads were a series of steel stampings gas-welded together. The head had an internal thread and screwed over the upper end of the cylinder against the topmost rib. The head was then welded in place to the top rib of the cylinder barrel. The water jacket was constructed from three 18-gauge sheet-steel stampings. The stampings were welded together, to the lowest rib on the cylinder, and to the screwed-on head, completing the jacket. Corrugations were pressed into the jacket at mid-length to take up differences in expansion and contraction between the cylinder and jacket as well as to stiffen the jacket wall. The head had two spark plugs on the centerline angled at 45° fore and aft from vertical.

Three valves per cylinder, another first for Duesenberg, were operated by the usual Duesenberg walking beam valve gear located in the Vee of the engine; however, the rocker arms were much shorter than normal because the single camshaft was mounted higher in the Vee than it had been on previous Duesenberg engines. The rocker arms were made of chrome-nickel steel forgings, had hardened steel rollers acting as cam followers, and were mounted on a hollow, stationary pivot shaft. The rocker arm pivot shaft was mounted to the top of the camshaft housing, which was a dust and oil-proof enclosure that ran the length of the engine and contributed to its rigidity when in place. The camshaft housing also had provisions for a vertical, Delco-designed generator driven from the camshaft bevel gear. The camshaft was an integral forging with a main diameter of 1 1/4" and was supported by eight babbitt-lined aluminum bearings.

The camshaft was driven by a vertical shaft at the rear of the engine. This vertical shaft was driven by the crankshaft and at the same speed. The vertical shaft was supported by annular ball bearings and had bevel gears at both top and bottom. The 2:1 reduction required for the camshaft was obtained at the upper end of the vertical shaft. Here, a small pinion on the vertical shaft meshed with a bevel gear on the camshaft with twice the number of teeth. The bevel pinion at the upper end of the shaft and the bevel gear on the camshaft were secured in place by means of splined joints. Both the pinion and bevel gear had long hubs where the inner races for the supporting ball bearings were mounted. The bevel gear at the lower end of the vertical shaft was forged integral with the shaft. Near its lower end, the vertical shaft carried a helical gear that meshed with another helical gear on a cross shaft to drive the two Dixie magnetos. The magnetos were set on mounts cast integral with the crankcase.

For each of the 16 cylinders, there was a single intake valve over a pair of exhaust valves, all exposed, located toward the Vee of the engine.

*Sectional view of the vertical drive shafts at the rear of the Model H. The **crankshaft** (1) drove the **upper vertical shaft** (2) that drove the **cross shaft for the magnetos** (3) and the **camshaft** (4). Below the crankshaft, the **lower vertical shaft** (5) drove the **oil pump** (6) and the **water pump** (7).*

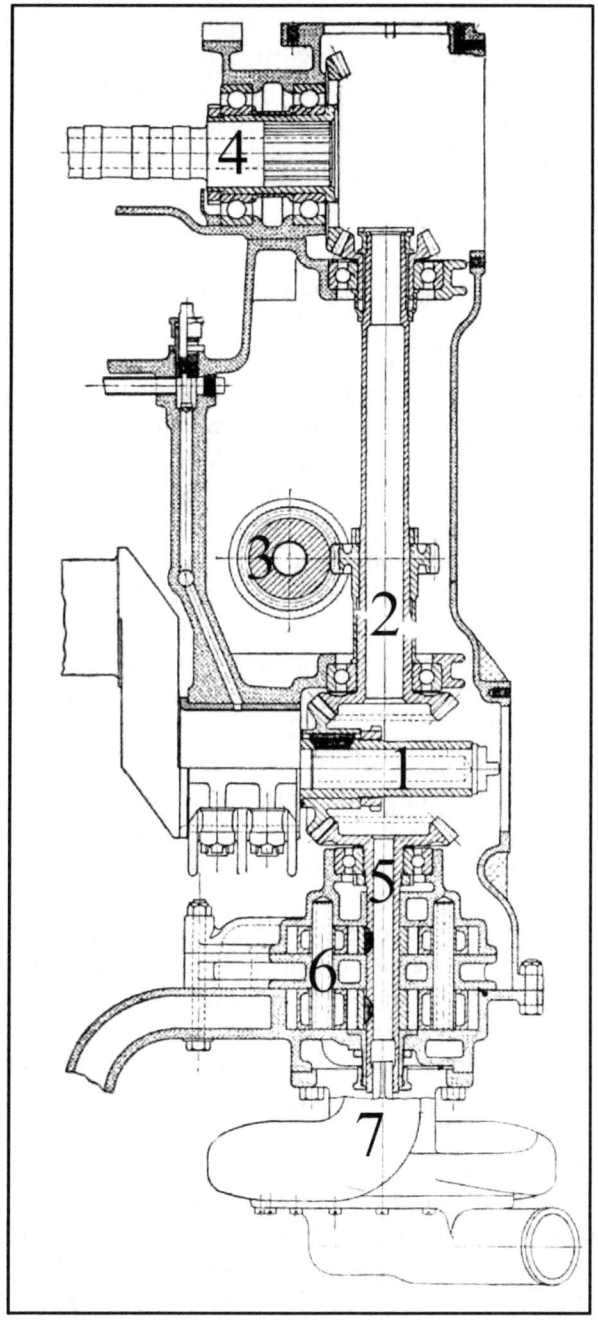

This layout allowed the incoming air to cool the exhaust valves while the exhaust valves heated the incoming air for better combustion. All valves had 30° seats. The intake valve had a throat diameter of 2 15/16", was lifted 9/16", and was 6 7/8" long. The two exhaust valves each had a throat diameter of 2 3/16", were lifted 1/2", and were 6 27/32" long. Each valve had two springs that, when the valve was closed, exerted 60 lb of combined pressure on each exhaust valve and 70 lb on the intake valve. Each valve was actuated by a rocker arm, and each rocker arm was actuated separately by the camshaft. Each valve could be removed by unscrewing the corresponding plug on the opposite side of the cylinder.

Each pair of adjacent cylinders had overlapping lugs on the cylinder heads. A bolt passed through the lugs to tie the two cylinders together. This connection stiffened the cylinders overall and reduced the side thrust from the piston on the individual cylinder. In addition, each pair of opposite cylinders were tied together by two steel stampings. These stampings were clamped to the lugs on the cylinder head exhaust stack flanges. A stamping was placed above and below the lugs, and bolts passed through both the stampings and the lugs. Each cylinder had two exhaust stacks extending vertically above the cylinder and positioned toward the Vee of the engine. Completed, each cylinder weighed 22 lb.

The cast Magnalite aluminum pistons were ribbed inside for strength and to transfer heat from the piston crown to the piston skirt. The piston was 5 1/4" long and had a 1 1/2" diameter wrist pin. Each piston had one 1/2" wide, three-piece piston ring. The ring was 7/8" below the top of the piston. The connecting rods were of the fork-and-blade type, had tubular sections, and were 12 3/4" long. The upper end of the rod was clamped by a screw through a split lug on the top of the rod.

The chrome-nickel steel forged crankshaft had eight throws. The four throws at one end were at right angles to the four at the other end. The crankshaft was supported by four plain bearings and by one ball bearing at the front (propeller end). All bearings were 2 7/8" in diameter and 3" long. The plain bearings had Non-Gran bronze shells with babbitt lining. The total weight of the crankshaft was 199 lb.

From experience with the V-12, Duesenberg had learned that closely spaced, large holes for the cylinders weakened the crankcase structure, and to compensate for this, the case was made of the barrel type. The individual cylinders were positioned in pairs. The paired cylinders were 7 1/8" apart at center. The non-paired cylinders were 9" apart at center. The crankcase casting's bottom was left open and was closed by means of a shallow aluminum base plate that made up the oil pan. This base plate, along with the camshaft and rocker arm housing mentioned earlier, stiffened the crankcase. The propeller end of the crankcase was also left open and was closed by a ribbed steel end-plate, mentioned earlier, that housed the bearings for the gear reduction.

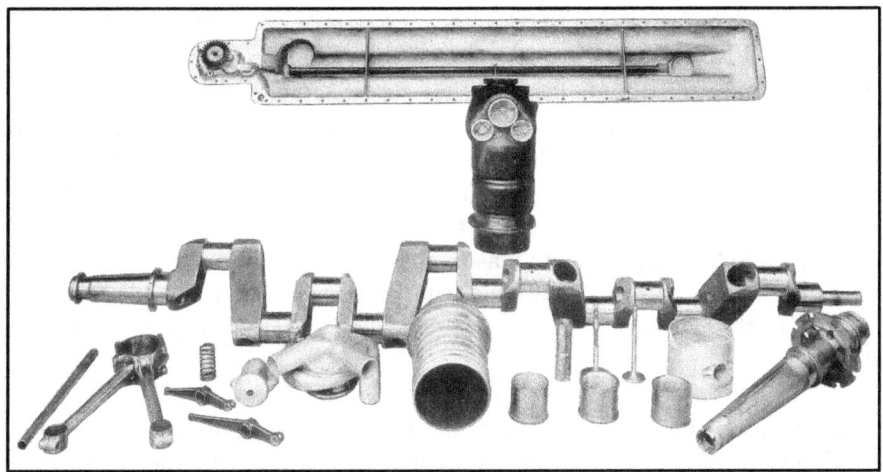

From top: oil pan with oil pump on the left, complete cylinder, crankshaft, rocker arm pivot shaft, fork-and-blade connecting rod, valve spring and rockers (exhaust is shorter), crankcase breather, water pump, cylinder barrel, three crankshaft bearings with a wrist pin behind, intake and exhaust valves (exhaust is shorter), piston, and the propeller shaft for the engine with gear reduction.

Camshaft and crankcase housing for the Model H with gear reduction.

There were circular access holes along both sides of the crankcase. On the left side, these holes were closed with cast cover plates; a series of crankcase breathers covered the holes on the right side. There were box girder partitions in the crankcase at each intermediate crankshaft bearing and substantial arch-shaped ribs midway between these box girders. The inside panels of the case's lower portion had diagonal or cross ribs to add to the strength of the case. A flange to support the engine in the aircraft fuselage was cast on each side of the case at the height of the crankshaft axis. The weight of the crankcase casing when machined was 180 lb.

The oil pump was mounted at the rear of the engine, below the crankshaft, and inside the crankcase oil pan. The water pump was mounted on the outside of the oil pan, directly below the oil pump. Both the oil pump and the water pump were driven at crankshaft speed through the same vertical drive shaft that extended below the crankshaft. This drive shaft was connected to the oil pump and was integrally forged with the driving bevel gear. The drive shaft for the oil and water pumps was in line with the drive shaft for the camshaft and magnetos, but the two shafts were not connected.

The dry sump lubrication system consisted of a two-section oil pump. One section was a triple-gear feed pump and the other a scavenging pump. The delivery pump forced oil to each main bearing through a single main oil line fitted into the crankcase. The main distributing line was fitted into the crankcase with packing glands; this was necessary because of the comparatively high oil pressure employed for the time, which rose to 75 psi when the engine ran at full speed.

A tube containing a regulator that reduced the oil pressure was taken off at the valve drive end of the main oil distributing line. This low pressure line extended along the top of the crank chamber, and from it there were two upward passages: one to the hollow camshaft and one to the hollow rocker pivot shaft. The excess oil from the rocker pivot shaft dropped onto the camshaft and ensured effective lubrication of the cams and rollers. The oil from the ends of the hollow camshaft returned through the reduction gear case at the front of the engine and through the housing of the vertical shaft at the rear of the engine. There was a dam at the vertical drive shaft end that determined the oil level in the camshaft housing. There were also passages through the cylinder flanges and cylinder walls; oil was injected through these passages and into the lower part of the cylinders to ensure their lubrication.

A tube from the low pressure distributing pipe extended through the upper part of the crankcase and into the gear reduction case. This tube had three lateral outlets opposite the reduction gear so that there was a constant supply of oil to the gear teeth as they came in contact. There was also a constant supply of oil in the bottom of the gear reduction case. The height of this oil was determined by the ball bearing on the end of the crankshaft.

The scavenging pump drew oil through large-size strainers at each end of the crankcase. The two inlet pipes allowed the scavenging pump to drain the crankcase no matter which direction the engine was inclined.

The crankpin bearings got their oil supply through passages drilled through the crankshaft from the main bearings, which received direct pressure lubrication. Oil for the crankpin bearing closest to the propeller end had to pass from the nearest intermediate bearing through a short crank arm, a crankpin, and a long crank arm.

Water was used as the coolant, and it was circulated through the cooling system from the centrifugal pump, located at the bottom rear of the engine. The pump turned at crankshaft speed and fed cooling water to the engine via two 1 7/8" diameter outlet tubes, one feeding each bank of cylinders. The water entered the jackets of the cylinder heads through welded water distributors that separated the flow into three streams. Each exhaust valve had its own stream leading directly beneath the exhaust port. The third stream led to the outside of the cylinder jacket. Water was taken out of the cylinder through an opening at the top of the cylinder. In addition to the regular water return connection, there was an

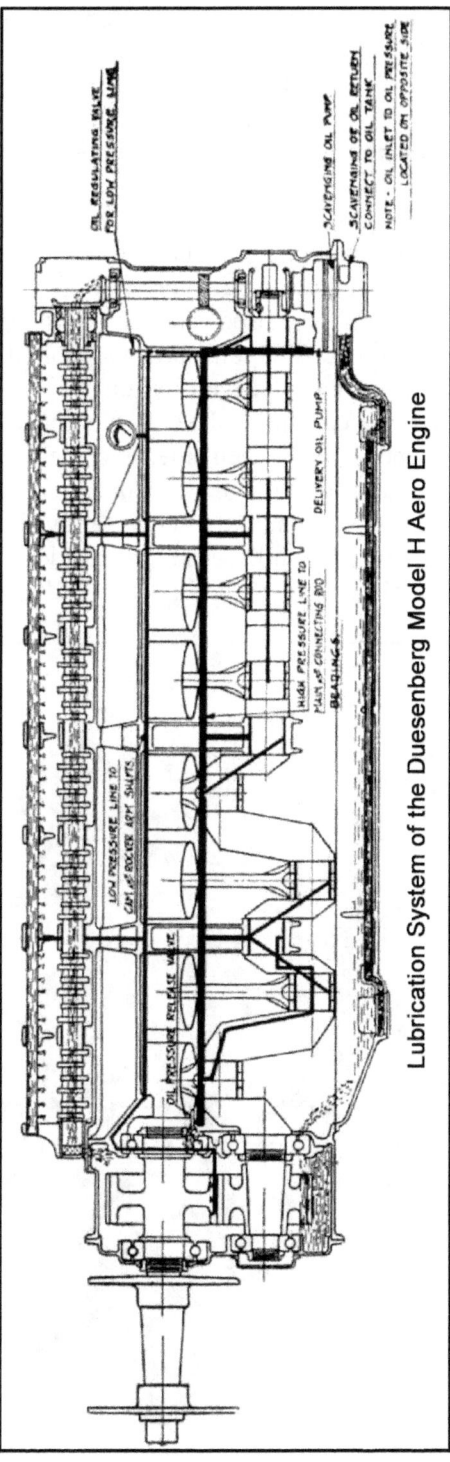

Lubrication System of the Duesenberg Model H Aero Engine

outlet connection at the bottom of each cylinder jacket to prevent dead spaces from forming in the cooling jacket. The intake manifolds were water-jacketed, and the water leaving the cylinder jackets passed through the jackets of the intake manifolds and then to the radiator. The water inlet temperature was 125° F, and the outlet temperature was 155° F.

The engines were equipped with both magnetos and battery ignition. Two eight-lead Dixie magnetos were fitted to the rear of the engine and driven from the upper vertical drive shaft. The mountings permitted any standard magnetos to be used. The battery ignition used a Delco distributor directly in line with the camshaft and bolted to the vertical shaft housing. The distributor was driven by an integral key engaging a transverse slot cut into the camshaft. The distributor was double-sided, with eight cables extending from each side. Each cable fired one of the spark plugs in each cylinder. The magnetos fired the other spark plug. A Philbrin battery ignition system with a generator turning at twice crankshaft speed was also tested successfully. The firing order was as follows: 4L, 1R, 8L, 5R, 2L, 3R, 6L, 7R, 1L, 4R, 5L, 8R, 3L, 2R, 7L, 6R.

Rear view of the Model H on a test stand. The manifold extending to the top of the image is the water coolant line to take hot water away from the engine. The double-sided distributor can be seen in the middle of the image. Below the distributor and mounted on the sides of the vertical shaft housing are the two magnetos. At the bottom rear of the engine is the Christensen self-starter that fed the left bank of cylinders.

Front view of the Model H with gear reduction on a test stand.

The fuel mixture was provided by four 2 1/4" Miller updraft carburetors, two on each side, located on the outside of the engine; each carburetor fed four cylinders. The two carburetors on the left side were clamped directly to footings on the crankcase, one toward the front of the engine and the other near the rear. The two carburetors on the right side were attached to an air duct that was fastened to a single footing in the center of the crankcase. Directly behind each footing was a passageway that extended through the width of the crankcase above each intermediate main crank bearing. Air flowed through these passageways to the carburetors and cooled the main crank bearings while being heated as it traveled to the carburetors. To take advantage of the ram air effect created by the aircraft's speed, it was intended for air ducts to extend forward from the engine to outside the fuselage of the aircraft. These ducts would feed air directly to the ends of the passageways, through the crankcase, and on to the carburetors.

The Model H engine was to be used with a Christensen self-starter. This unit was located on the rear of the engine and mounted in line with the crankshaft. The air/fuel mixture from the starter was fed at 150 psi into the left bank of cylinders through one of the two removable plugs for exhaust valve access.

Beginning in June of 1918, the engine was run extensively in the Duesenberg engine test house. Test stand engine runs included the use of a 16-foot test club propeller. Dynamometer engine runs were accomplished by spinning three 300-400 hp Sprague Electric dynamometers coupled together. It was believed that fuel consumption could be held within 0.56 lb/hp/hr, and the oil consumption was noted as very light. The engine showed remarkable acceleration, and torque was observed to be very steady throughout a wide rpm range when under test on the dynamometer. Reportedly, the geared drive Model H was ready for its official test on December 31, 1918, but no full power readings were ever made because the engine had considerable trouble and ultimately failed due to a structural weakness before the runs were completed. It was thought that 900 hp was obtainable at higher engine speeds.

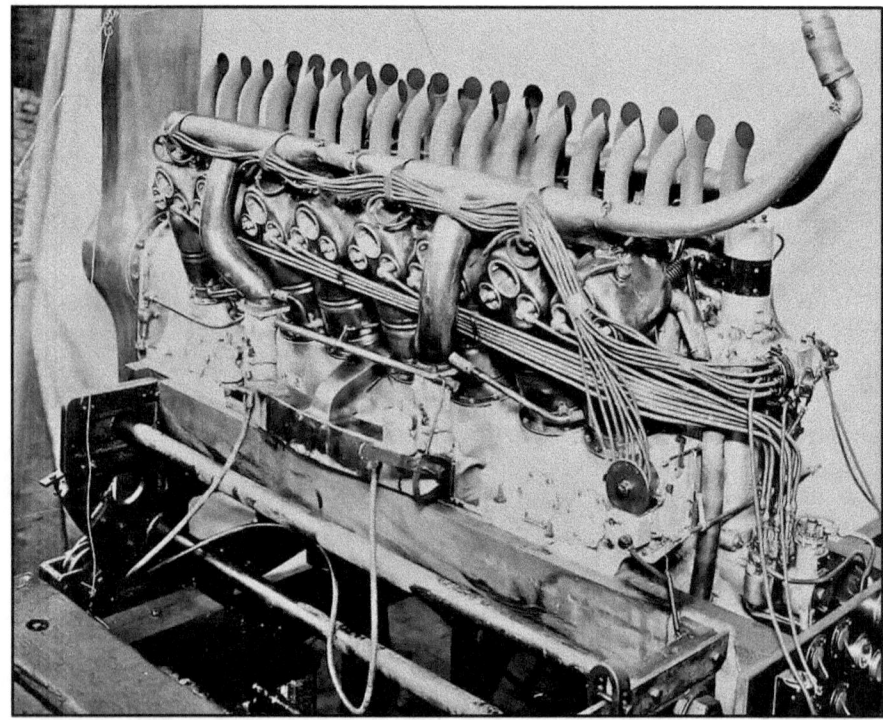

Rear 3/4 view showing the installation of the Christensen self-starter, magneto, and distributor to advantage. The left side of the engine had access cover plates rather than crankcase breathers. The two carburetors were attached to a common air duct that was mounted to the middle footing / air passageway on the crankcase.

7. Duesenberg Model H V-16 Engine

Due to its length, this giant Duesenberg aircraft engine would not fit into any existing aircraft, and no aircraft was produced to hold the engine. With the end of World War I and the trouble with the engine during testing, the contract for further development was dropped, ending Duesenberg's involvement with aircraft engines.

An engine with an output of over 800 hp was a very ambitious endeavor. Late in 1918, very few engines could produce that much power, and perhaps none could exceed it. But what was probably most impressive about the Model H was its weight when compared to its displacement and power. While some engine manufactures simply combined two existing engines to produce a high-powered engine, Duesenberg started from scratch to design a world-class engine. The Model H achieved less than two pounds per horsepower, which was a very respectable figure for that time period. Compared to the King-Bugatti, the Model H had twice the displacement and twice the power for only 26 percent additional weight. Coming in at 2.00 lb/hp, even the Liberty V-12, which was considered the cutting edge of engine science and art for its time, could not beat the Model H's specific weight of 1.97 lb/hp. Jumping ahead to the 1930s for a comparison, the Model H's displacement was near that of the Allison V-3420, while its weight was close to the Allison V-1710.

Right side view of the Model H with gear reduction on a test stand. The right side of the engine had the crankcase breathers and the carburetors mounted directly to the front and rear footings / air passageways on the crankcase. The middle air passageway through the crankcase is visible.

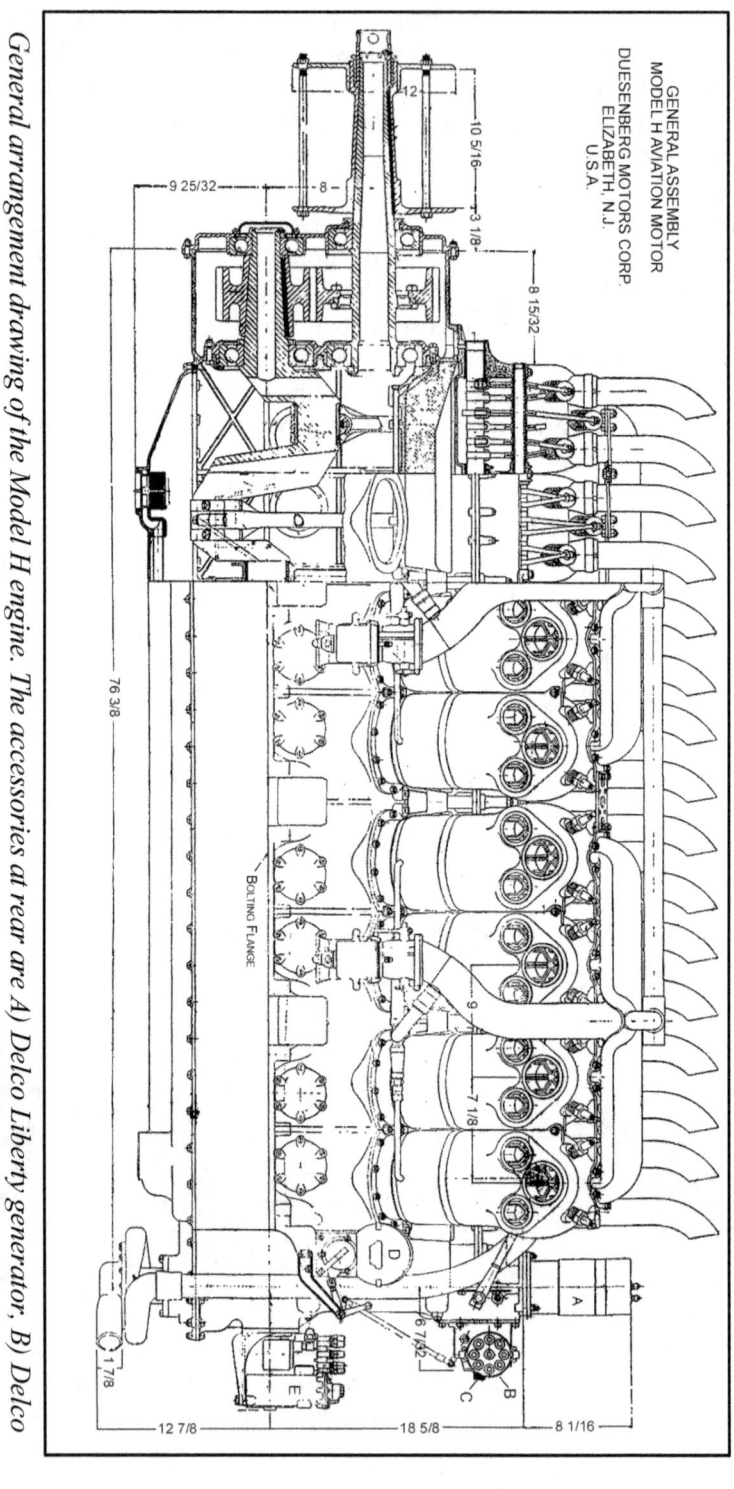

General arrangement drawing of the Model H engine. The accessories at rear are A) Delco Liberty generator, B) Delco distributor, C) tachometer drive, D) Dixie magneto, and E) Christensen self-starter. Note the cylinder spacing.

7. Duesenberg Model H V-16 Engine

Model H hooked up to the three Sprague dynamometers in the Duesenberg engine test house.

Engine Specifications

Engine:	Model H (Specifically, H-1 was the geared version and H-2 was the direct drive version.)
First Run:	1918
Type:	45° V-16, three valves per cylinder, water-cooled, aircraft engine
Horsepower:	Direct 700 hp at 1,550 rpm
	Geared 800 hp at 1,800 rpm
Displacement:	3,393 in^3
Bore:	6"
Stroke:	7.5"
Compression Ratio:	4.66:1
BMEP:	Direct 105.4 psi, Geared 103.7 psi
Specific Weight:	Direct 1.99 lb/hp, Geared 1.97 lb/hp
Specific Power:	Direct 0.21 hp/in^3, Geared 0.24 hp/in^3
Gear Reduction:	None or 0.758:1
Carburetion:	Four 2.25" Miller updraft
Firing order:	4L, 1R, 8L, 5R, 2L, 3R, 6L, 7R, 1L, 4R, 5L, 8R, 3L, 2R, 7L, 6R
Length:	88.75"
Width:	32"
Height:	38.875"
Weight:	Direct 1,390 lb, Geared 1,575 lb

Duesenberg Model H on a test stand in the Duesenberg engine test house. The worker gives some perspective to the size of the engine.

Survivors

Amazingly, two Model H engines survive. While not complete, one engine is on display at the Auburn-Cord-Duesenberg Automobile Museum in Auburn, Indiana, which was once the Duesenberg national headquarters. This engine is a geared drive version and, including display stand, was part of the Frank Srp estate sold at auction in late April 1969. The engine and stand were donated to the museum by Dee and Georgia Howard of San Antonio, Texas. After World War II, Dee Howard converted surplus Lockheed Venturas into executive transport aircraft, which he named *Super Venturas*. This line of aircraft ultimately led to the *Howard 500*. In the Jet Age, Howard developed thrust reversers and various performance upgrades for business aircraft. Dee Howard was an avid car collector and had amassed a large assortment of Duesenberg engine and automotive parts. He passed away on February 12, 2009.

The other surviving engine is a direct drive version and is in storage at the National Air and Space Museum's Garber Facility in Silver Hill, Maryland. The engine appears to be nearly complete; it even includes the Christensen self-starter, magnetos, generator, distributor, intake manifolds, and carburetors. However, it is missing the air duct for the two carburetors on the right side of the engine.

7. Duesenberg Model H V-16 Engine

Right side of the Model H as displayed at the Auburn-Cord-Duesenberg Automobile Museum in Auburn, Indiana. Of note are the crankcase breathers and the air passageways through the crankcase.

Bottom view from the left rear of the Model H showing the engine mounting flange that was cast the entire length of the crankcase. Also visible is the oil pan and how it is attached to the crankcase. Note the footings to mount the carburetors to the air passageways through the crankcase (Martt Clupper photos via AirPigz, www.airpigz.com).

75

Opposite page—Rear view of the Model H displaying the compact design of the 45° V-16 engine. The circular cover in-line with the camshaft is where the double-sided distributor mounted. The flat horizontal mounts on each side of the crankcase are for the magnetos. The circular cover in-line with the crankshaft is for the Christensen self-starter. Also visible is the auxiliary water outlet connection at the bottom of each cylinder water jacket and the crankcase breathers on the right side of the engine (Martt Clupper photo via AirPigz, www.airpigz.com).

Left rear 3/4 view of the engine as displayed at the Auburn-Cord-Duesenberg Automobile Museum. A good view is provided of the circular access covers on the crankcase. Note the magneto drive mid-way along the vertical drive shaft housing and the horizontal magneto mount cast into the crankcase (Martt Clupper photo via AirPigz, www.airpigz.com).

View of the walking beam rocker arms for the 48 valves. Note the steel stampings tying opposite cylinders together. The second one from bottom is missing (Martt Clupper photo via AirPigz, www.airpigz.com).

A view looking down the Vee of the Model H. The plate in the foreground is where the generator would mount (Martt Clupper photo via AirPigz, www.airpigz.com).

7. *Duesenberg Model H V-16 Engine*

Another look at the 48 rocker arms exuding a level of elegance, sophistication, and complication that is not seen in modern engines (Martt Clupper photo via AirPigz, www.airpigz.com).

The Model H engine of 1918 was truly a work of beauty (Martt Clupper photo via AirPigz, www.airpigz.com).

Close up view of the cylinder top. Note the water jacket welds and the overlapping lugs that tie the adjacent cylinders together on the right. The plate on the top of each cylinder is where the intake manifold would attach (Martt Clupper photo via AirPigz, www.airpigz.com).

The nearly complete direct drive Model H engine in storage at the National Air and Space Museum's Garber Facility in Silver Hill, Maryland (Photo © 2010 Fred van der Horst, via the Aircraft Engine Historical Society, www.enginehistory.com).

Epilogue

Duesenberg Motors Corporation had spent much of its capital on its facilities in New Jersey and on the development of aircraft engines. Once WWI ended and the government contracts were cancelled, the company found itself in financial distress. Duesenberg ceased development of aircraft engines, and the company was reorganized.

Duesenberg Motors Corporation filed a breach of contract lawsuit against the U.S. government, alleging that the government did not provide the necessary information for a production-ready Bugatti engine. Duesenberg lost the case on the grounds that the government was unaware the Bugatti engine was not ready for production and was rightly more concerned with ending the war than producing the engine.

While none of the Duesenberg aircraft engines achieved any level of commercial success, they do occupy a level of historical importance for their unique features. The enclosed and well lubricated valve gear used on most of their engines stands out as a viable solution to the valve issues that plagued early aircraft engines. And while many engines got by with splash lubrication, Duesenberg's use of pressure lubrication is another example of their understanding of what was needed to ensure reliable, high-powered engines. The quality of the engines and the thoroughness of the designs turned out by the small Duesenberg design department give a glimpse of the inherent genius of Fred Duesenberg.

As an anecdotal note on born intuition versus learned calculation, before his death in 1932, Fred Duesenberg was shown the prototype Allison V-1710 at the Allison Engineering Company plant in Indianapolis, Indiana. Duesenberg liked the design but commented that he felt the crankshaft seemed a little weak to his eye. The Allison engineers assured him that the design had been carefully calculated and that it had ample strength. But during tests of the V-1710, it was found that the crankshaft needed to be redesigned and strengthened to cure vibration issues.

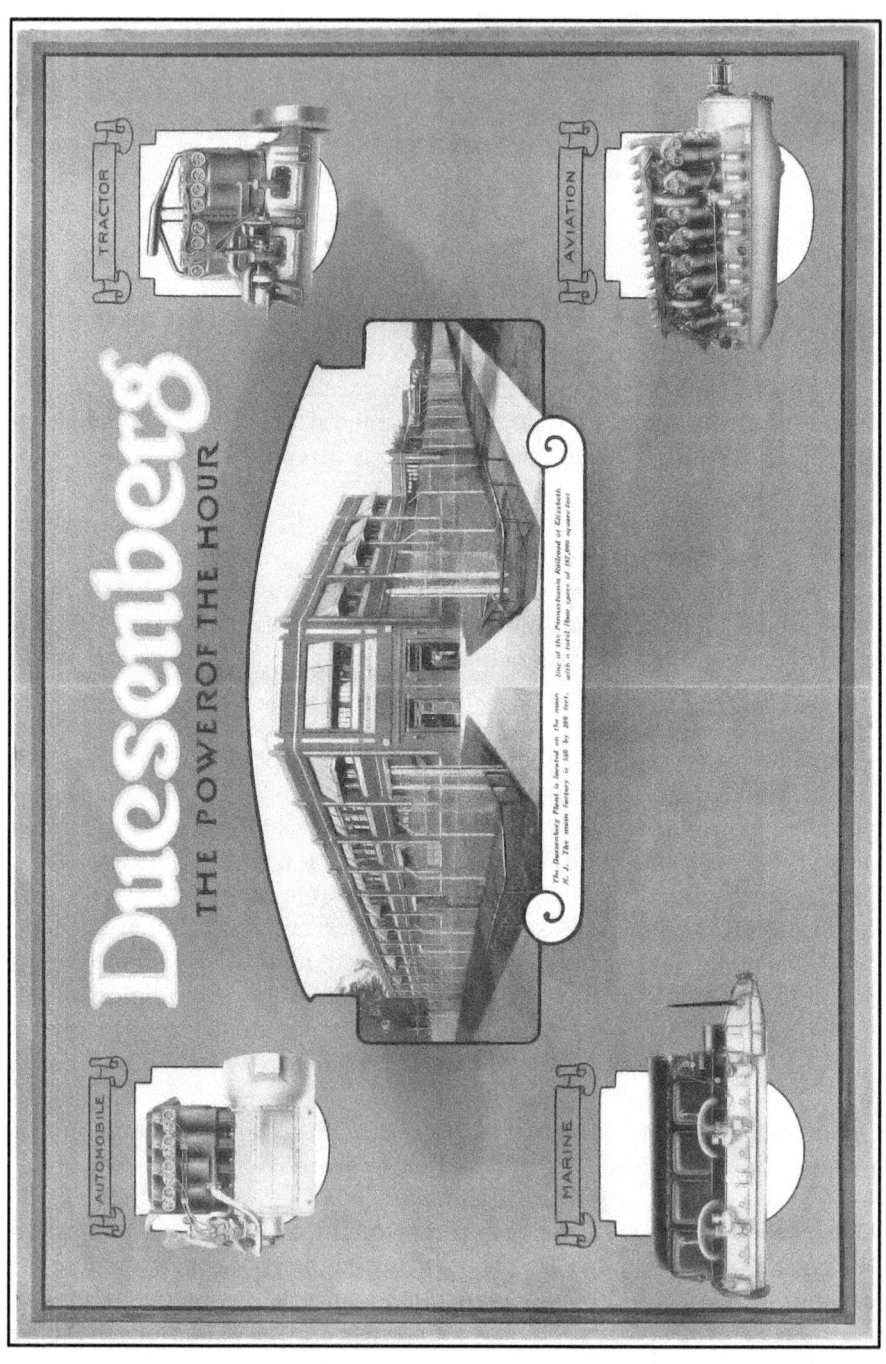

Appendix A – Duesenberg Aircraft Engine Comparison

	Special A	Special A3	V-12	16-v, Straight-4	King-Bugatti	Model H
Engine Type:	Straight-4	Straight-4	60° V-12	Straight-4	U-16	45° V-16
First Run:	1915	1915	1916	1916	1918	1918
Horsepower:		70 / 85	300 / 350	D 100 / G 140	410	D 700 / G 800
RPM:		1,500 / 2,220	1,400 / 1,800	D 1,500 / G 2,100	2,000	D 1,550 / G 1,800
Displacement (in³):	299	361	1,568	496	1,484	3,393
Bore (in):	3.984	4.375	4.875	4.75	4.33	6
Stroke (in):	6	6	7	7	6.3	7.5
Compression Ratio:					5:1	4.66:1
Valves Per Cylinder:	2	2	2	4	3	3
BMEP (psi):		102.4 / 84.0	108.2 / 98.2	D 106.5 / G 106.5	109.4	D 105.4 / G 103.7
Specific Weight (lb/hp):		5.21 / 4.29	3.47 / 2.97	D 4.36 / G 3.64	3.04	D 1.99 / G 1.97
Specific Power (hp/in³):		0.19 / 0.24	0.19 / 0.22	D 0.20 / G 0.25	0.28	D 0.21 / G 0.24
Gear Reduction:	None	None	None	None or 0.579:1	0.667:1	None or 0.758:1
Carburation:	Miller x1	Miller x1	Miller x1 or x2	Miller x1	Miller x4	Miller x4
Length (in):			68	43.375	44.25	88.75
Width (in):			31.25	15.5	24.8	32
Height (in):			39.625	37.5	32.28	38.875
Weight (lb):	365	365	1,040	D 436 / G 509	1,248	D 1,390 / G 1,575

D = Direct Drive
G = Geared Drive
/ = Used to separate different values representative of different rpm and hp output for the same engine, or direct drive from geared drive.

Duesenberg wartime ad from 1918.

Appendix B – Duesenberg Valve Gear Patent

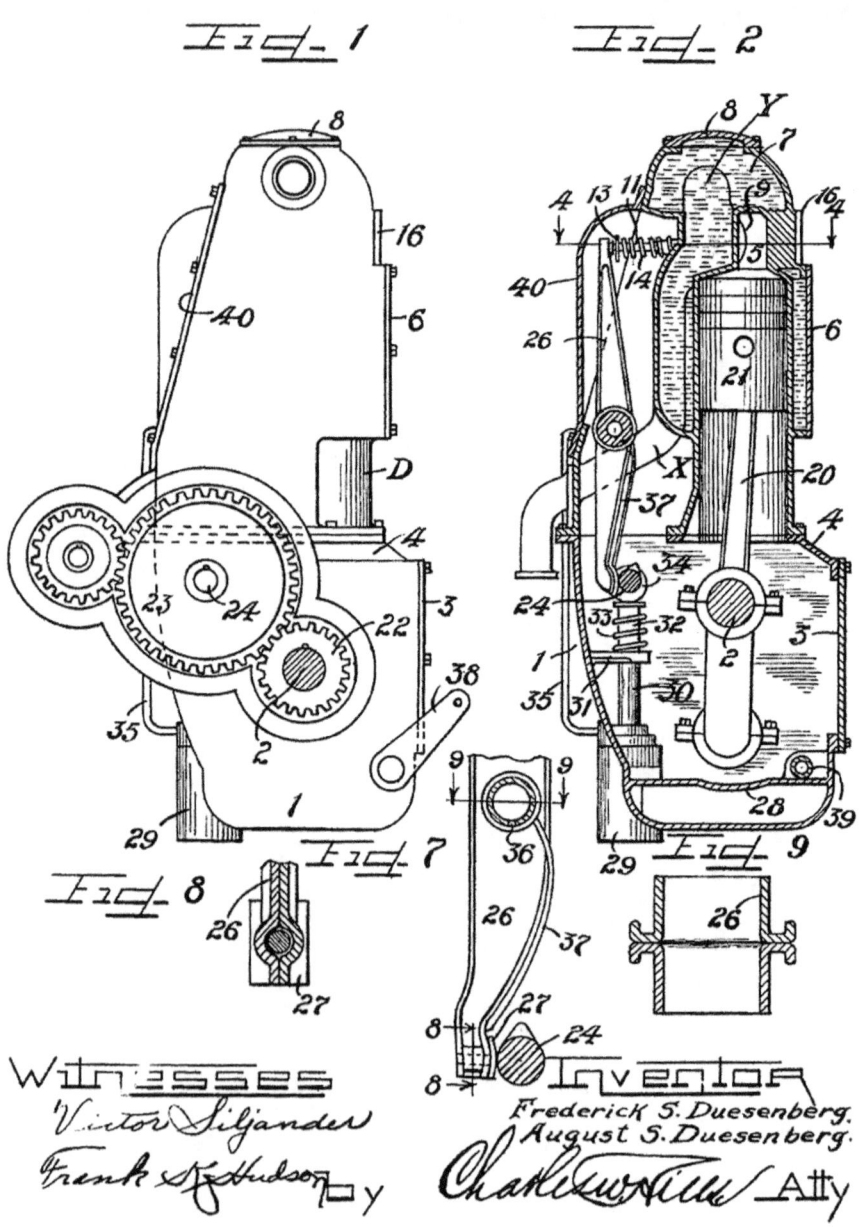

Appendix B – Duesenberg Valve Gear Patent

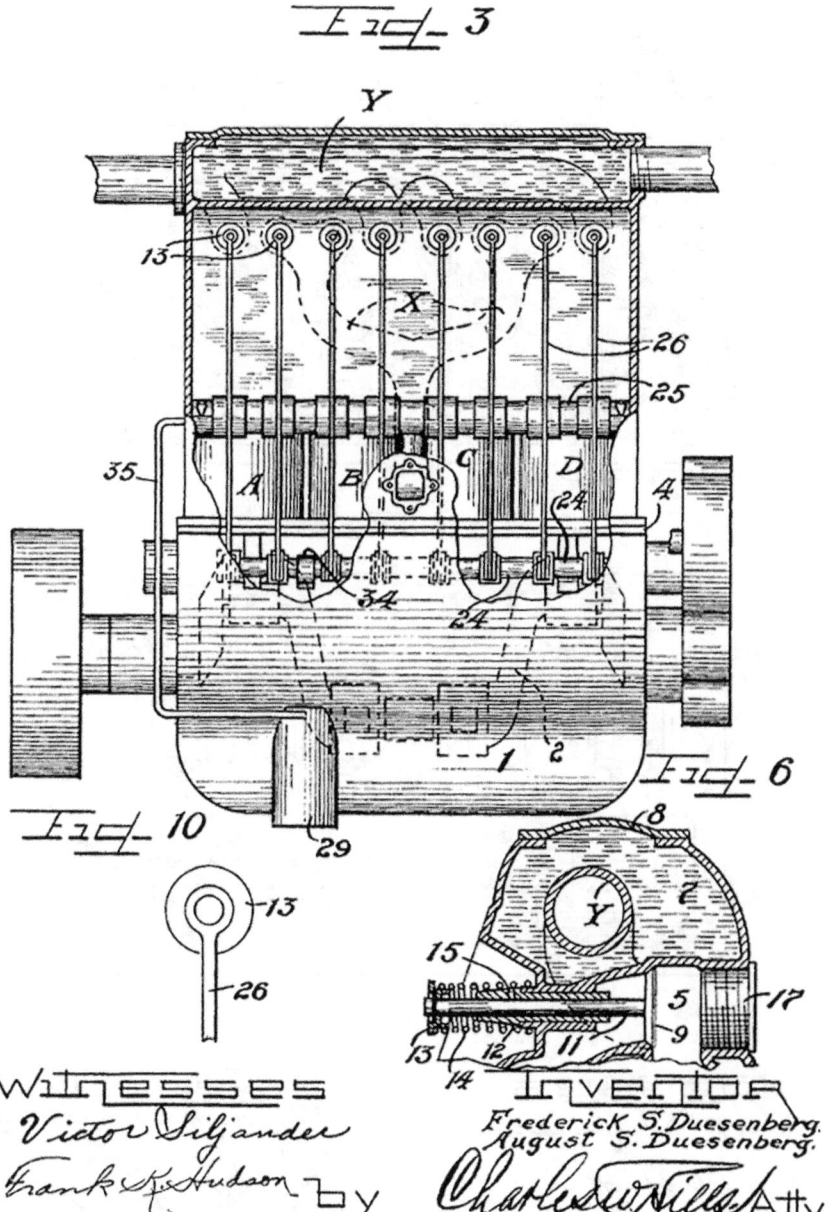

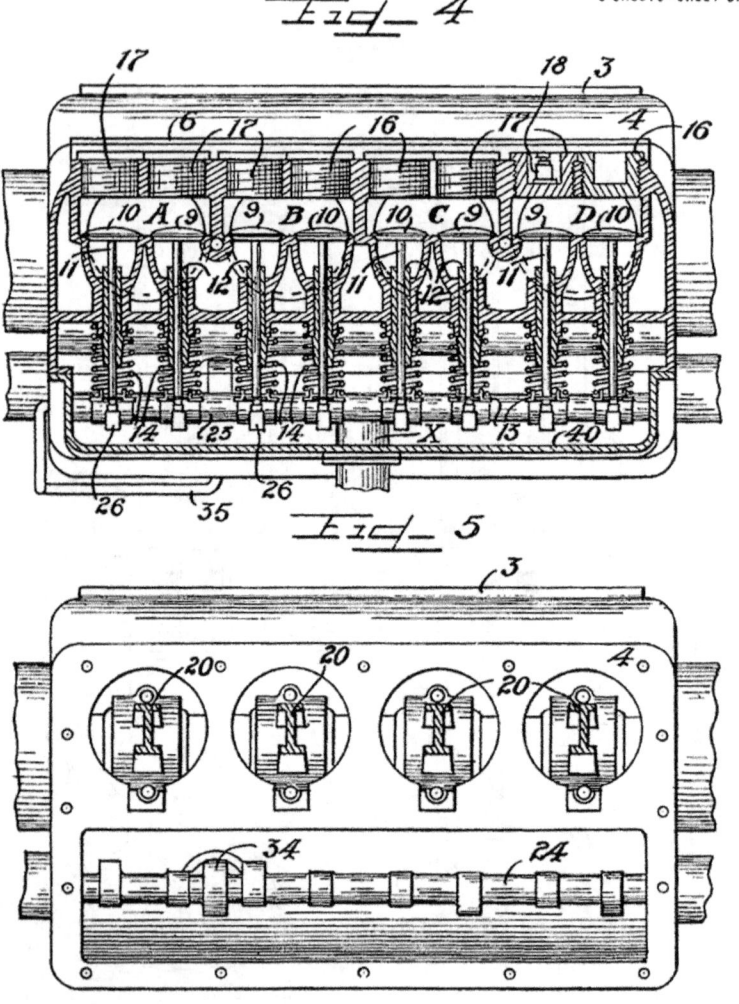

UNITED STATES PATENT OFFICE.

FREDERICK S. DUESENBERG AND AUGUST S. DUESENBERG, OF DES MOINES, IOWA.

VALVE-GEAR.

1,244,481.   Specification of Letters Patent.   **Patented Oct. 30, 1917.**

Original application filed April 14, 1913, Serial No. 760,851. Divided and this application filed August 13, 1914. Serial No. 856,543.

To all whom it may concern:

Be it known that we, FREDERICK S. DUESENBERG and AUGUST S. DUESENBERG, a subject of the Emperor of Germany and a citizen of the United States, respectively, and both residents of the city of Des Moines, county of Polk, and State of Iowa, have invented certain new and useful Improvements in Valve-Gears; and we do hereby declare that the following is a full, clear, and exact description of the same, reference being had to the accompanying drawings, and to the numerals of reference marked thereon, which form a part of this specification.

This invention relates to an improved valve gear particularly well adapted for use on internal combustion engines, although, of course, not limited to such, being a divisional application of our co-pending application for patent for "internal combustion engines", filed April 14th, 1913, Serial No. 760,851.

Much of the inefficiency of gas engines now upon the market wherein puppet valves are used, may be traced to the valve action, owing to the fact that at high speed the valves do not seat perfectly. Furthermore, due to the fact that the valves are in a position on the cylinder subject to the heat of the explosion, they become overheated and stick open, and then too they become fouled with carbon forming a product of the combustion. In internal combustion engines heretofore constructed an exceedingly large clearance space has been practically unavoidable where it is desired to use large valves, and this is particularly true of the well known type of T-head motor. Another disadvantageous feature in prior constructions has been that the fuel entering through the valves has been required to flow a considerable distance before reaching the ignition means and the time required for such travel is an important factor when the motor is operating at high speed. It is almost essential that the fuel be ignited immediately upon its admission after closure of the admission valve, so closely and quickly do the events in the cycle of operation take place.

Another defect in multi-cylinder engines has been the complication of valve mechanisms with an inadequate lubricating system therefor, but which, in our invention, is a feature of the valve gear which has been carefully considered.

It is an object of this invention to construct an upright internal combustion engine with valves opening horizontally into a small clearance space above the cylinders thereof, and with an improved valve gear for actuating the valves in proper sequence.

It is also an object of this invention to construct an internal combustion engine provided with water jacketed valves opening laterally into a small clearance space above the cylinders and with mechanism for actuating said valves incased within the engine, concealed from view, and protected, as well as insuring a silent running engine.

It is also an object of this invention to construct an internal combustion engine wherein a valve gear is provided for the laterally movable valves embracing a plurality of rocker arms, one for each valve and actuated by a suitable cam shaft, and with a lubricating means associated with the valve gear and operated from a part thereof to admit oil to the wearing surfaces of the gear.

It is a further object of this invention to construct a valve gear for the valves of an internal combustion engine wherein certain members of the valve gear mechanism serve to convey lubricating oil therethrough, and with means associated with said member to intermittently communicate with the oil carrying means to feed the oil to other parts of the gear.

It is finally an object of this invention to provide in combination with an internal combustion engine of novel construction, a particularly efficient valve gear incased within the walls of the engine and well lubricated at all points, and connected to be driven from the crank shaft of the engine.

The invention (in a preferred form) is illustrated in the drawings and hereinafter more fully described.

In the drawings:

Figure 1 is an end elevation of an engine embodying our invention, and with the cover for the gear case removed.

Fig. 2 is a vertical section thereof.

Fig. 3 is a left side elevation broken away and partly in section.

Fig. 4 is an enlarged fragmentary detail section taken on line 4—4 of Fig. 2.

Fig. 5 is an enlarged top plan view of the crank case with the cylinders removed and the connecting rods in section.

Fig. 6 is an enlarged fragmentary vertical

89

section taken through the top of the engine, illustrating the mounting of one of the valves therein.

Fig. 7 is an enlarged detail partly in section and partly in elevation of the lower end of one of the rocker arms and the cam shaft for actuating the same.

Fig. 8 is a detail section taken on line 8—8 of Fig. 7.

Fig. 9 is a detail section taken on line 9—9 of Fig. 7 with parts omitted.

Fig. 10 is a fragmentary rear view of the upper end of the rocker arm.

As shown in the drawings:

The crank case 1, is constructed of cast metal in any suitable manner, and is provided, if desired, with transverse interior webs, on which, and at the ends of the crank case is journaled the crank shaft 2, which may be constructed, of course, as usual, the construction in this particular as to the bearings for the crank shaft, varying with the size of the engine, and the number of cylinders employed. Said crank case is provided on its right side with a removable side plate to afford access to the interior of the crank case, and at its top is provided with a suitably apertured and seated base plate 4, which may be integral with the remainder of the crank case, if desired, and upon which seat and are rigidly secured the respective cylinders A, B, C, and D, which are rigidly secured in place thereon in the usual or any suitable manner.

Said cylinders, as shown, are each provided at the top with a relatively narrow and upwardly extending combustion chamber 5, which communicates in the top of the cylinder and extends substantially parallel the crank shaft, and the top of the cylinder is so shaped as to afford a slight clearance above the piston when at the end of its exhaust, and its compression strokes.

Each of said cylinders is water jacketed, and the water jacket may be afforded by coring the cylinder when cast or in any suitable manner. Conveniently, on the right or ignition side of said engine, a removable plate 6, affords one wall of the water jacket, and by removal permits access to the interior of the water jacket for inspection or repair. For the remaining portion of the periphery of the cylinder, and extending well into the head thereof above and around the combustion chamber, the water jacket is preferably cored in the metal, as indicated by 7, and if desired, a cover plate 8, may be provided to afford access to the interior of the water jacket by its removal.

Inlet and exhaust ports of relatively large size are provided at the left side of the combustion chamber and are closed by mechanically operated puppet valves 9 and 10, respectively, each of which is rigidly secured on a stem 11, which extends through a suitable bearing sleeve 12, seated in a suitable bore in the side of the engine cylinder adjacent the combustion chamber, as shown in Figs. 4 and 6. Secured on the outer end of the valve stem 11, is a stop 13, between which and the wall of the cylinder engages a pushing spring 14, said spring acting at all times to hold its valve closed. As shown, an oil aperture is provided in the bearing sleeve 12, for each valve stem, and opens upwardly at the outer side of the sleeve, as indicated by 15, in Fig. 6, whereby the oil (converted practically to a vapor by the splash lubrication hereinafter described) finds access to the stem to lubricate the same at all times.

The inlet valves are arranged in pairs in adjacent cylinders. In the construction shown, in which four cylinders are used, the inlet valves 9, of the cylinders A and B, are closely adjacent each other, and between the exhaust valves for said cylinders, and in the cylinders C and D, the same arrangement is maintained, so that the inlet manifold X, indicated in dotted lines in Fig. 3, requires but two branches for a four cylinder engine, one of the branches opening directly to the valves 9, in the cylinders A and B, and the other of the same opening directly to the valves 9, in the cylinders C and D, while the exhaust manifold Y, as indicated also in dotted lines in Fig. 3, is provided with four branches which lead from the respective exhaust valves and upwardly therefrom.

The right side of the combustion chamber, or that opposite the valves, is bored to afford relatively large threaded openings therein, one directly opposite each of the valves and threaded thereinto are closures 16, for the exhaust valves, and 17, for the inlet valves, the latter of said closures being apertured to permit the insertion of a spark plug 18, in close proximity with the inlet valve and directed toward the axis thereof, as shown in Fig. 4. Said closures, upon removal, permit ready removal of the respective valves through the opening therefor, and permit the hand to be inserted into the cylinder to permit the cylinder to be thoroughly cleaned and any carbon therein removed, when desired, and without necessitating removing the cylinders from the crank case.

Connected with the respective cranks of the crank shaft, are connecting rods 20, of course, one for each cylinder, and each engaged with a piston 21, which may be constructed in the usual or any suitable manner. The crank shaft is provided on its outer end with a gear wheel 22, which meshes with a larger gear wheel 23, secured on a cam shaft 24, and affording a two to one drive therefor, said cam shaft being journaled in the crank case extending longitudinally at the rear side thereof, and provided with suitable cams for actuating the respective valves. Said gears are, of course, incased to permit the same to run in oil.

Journaled above the cam shaft, is a tubular shaft 25, journaled on which are rocker arms 26, each made up of abutting flat levers with reinforced edges and having a cylindrical extension integrally formed a short distance below the middle thereof to permit said rocker arms to be journaled on the shaft 25, one rocker arm for each inlet valve, and one for each exhaust valve, the upper, longer end of each of which extends into engagement with the outer end of the corresponding valve stem, as shown in Figs. 2 and 3, while the lower end thereof, which may be provided with a suitable anti-friction shoe 27, extends into bearing against the cam shaft in position to be engaged and actuated by the appropriate and corresponding cam thereon, so that when the shorter end of said lever is actuated by the cam, the upper end is thrown inwardly with greater velocity, instantly affording full opening of the valve actuated thereby, which, upon release of said rocker arm by said cam, is instantly closed by the action of the valve spring 14.

The bearing on said tubular shaft 25, for the rocker arm, is supplied with force feed lubrication; so also is the lower end of said rocker arm, so that the friction occasioned by the engagement of said rocker arms by the respective cams, is reduced to a minimum. For this purpose, as shown, an oil compartment is provided in the bottom of the crank case, an inner floor or bottom 28, being provided therein, as shown in Fig. 2, the space beneath said inner floor affording an oil well or container, and communicating therewith at the bottom, and cored in the side of the cylinder, is a casing 29, providing a cylindric bore or chamber therein in open communication with said oil compartment at its inner side.

A pump barrel 30, is held in position over said chamber 29, by a bracket 31, extending inwardly from the walls of the crank case, and slidable through said barrel 30, is a plunger 32, normally impelled upwardly by a spring 33, wound therearound, the upper end of said plunger bearing beneath a cam 34, secured on said cam shaft 24. A pipe 35, communicates in the bore of the tubular rocker arm shaft 25, and also with said pump chamber 29, so that the interior of said shaft is at all times filled with oil. At each bearing of the rocker arms on said shaft, an oil port 36, is provided for the rocker arm, and as clearly shown in Fig. 7, and connected in the hub of each of the rocker arms is a pipe or tube 37, which leads downwardly therefrom along the inner face of the rocker arm and delivers oil to the bearing plate 27, on the end of the rocker arm engaged by the cam.

Of course, the bearing plate or shoe 27, may be adjustably secured upon said rocker arm if desired, and also at the upper end adjustable means may be provided to vary the bearing of said arm on the valve stem. Conveniently also, and particularly in the larger engines, an anti-friction roller may be provided on the lower end of the rocker to minimize friction from engagement with the cam with the rocker for actuating the latter. This, in engines of smaller size, is, however, not necessary. A crank 38, on the end of the crank case, is connected to a valve element 39, journaled in the bottom of the crank case for controlling the level of the oil therein, but inasmuch as this mechanism forms no part of the present invention, the details of construction and operation thereof are not entered into here.

When the engine is assembled and properly adjusted a left side closing plate 40, is secured in place, as shown clearly in Figs. 1 and 2, to entirely inclose the rocker shaft, rocker arm, and all the operating or moving parts of the engine, the joints of course being preferably gasketed or ground to afford a tight fit and prevent leakage of oil.

The operation is as follows:

The entire left side of the crank case being open, the oil within the crank case is driven into a fine mist almost vaporous in character, which, at all times, bathes all the operating parts of the engine, affording efficient lubrication. The oil falling upon the valve stem 11, and passing into the oil port 15, in the sleeve 12, insures thorough lubrication for, as well as serving to cool the valve stem, and also lubrication for the point of engagement of the upper end of the rocker arm, with the end of the valve stem.

Owing to the hollow tubular shaft 25, through which oil is conveyed and on which the rocker arms are journaled, the bearings for the rocker arms are readily lubricated, so that minimum friction and resistance is afforded for the operation of the valves. The cam 34, on the cam shaft 24, serves to operate the plunger oil pump, pumping oil through the pipe 35, which communicates with the interior of said tubular shaft 25. Of course, the small pipes 37, mounted on each of the rocker arms, serve to intermittently receive oil from said tubular shaft 25, and feed the same to the contacting surfaces of the wear plates 27, and cams upon the cam shaft. The cycle of operation is as usual in four cylinder four stroke internal combustion engines. However, as the inlet manifold X, has but two branches of equal length, owing to the inlet valves of each pair of cylinders being provided adjacent each other, it follows that an equal supply of hydro-carbon mixture is provided for each cylinder, thus affording uniform and efficient operation.

The shape and position of the respective relatively high but narrow combustion chambers 5, arranged above the axis of each cylinder, is such that the inlet and exhaust valve of each cylinder at one side of the combustion chamber, are brought into very close relation with the ignition means, so that when the charge is compressed the ignition terminals are practically at the center of the compressed mixture. This is important, as it affords uniform and complete combustion of the entire charge almost instantaneously. Not only does the arrangement of the valves and spark plug add greatly to the efficiency of the engine, but a further and important advantage is found in the readiness with which the valves and the exterior of the cylinders may be inspected. The closures 16 and 17, may be removed when desired, thereby permitting the removal and replacement of the valves therethrough, and as well the combustion chamber may be cleaned when desired through said apertures.

Of course it is to be understood that details of construction will vary through a considerable degree with the size of the engine. For example, it is desirable to provide rollers on the cam ends of the rocker arms for large units, and in some instances force feed lubrication may be used elsewhere than as shown and described. We have, of course, shown a preferred form of our invention, but we do not purpose limiting the patent granted otherwise than necessitated by the prior art.

We claim as our invention:

1. In a device of the class described a multiple cylinder internal combustion engine embracing cylinders, pistons, a crank shaft, a continuously driven cam shaft, rocker arms journaled above the cam shaft with the shorter arms thereof directed into position for direct contact with the cams thereon, and the longer ends directed into position for valve actuation, inlet and exhaust valves arranged transversely the axis of the cylinder and at the same side of the cylinder, each provided with spring pressed stems extending into position each for direct contact with the rocker arms, and means mounted on the rocker arms and movable therewith for lubricating the bearings for the rocker arms and the points of engagement of the cams thereon.

2. In a device of the class described a multiple cylinder engine, inlet valves arranged in pairs for adjacent cylinders, an exhaust valve adjacent and parallel therewith for each cylinder, said valves acting transversely the axis of the cylinder, rocker arms journaled at the side of each cylinder for characteristically actuating the valves, a crank case open at the top at one side into which said rocker arms extend, end walls formed on the engine, and a cover plate attached thereon inclosing said rocker arms.

3. In a device of the class described the valves and valve stems, and mechanisms for operating the same embracing a bearing sleeve for each valve stem ported to permit admission of oil to the stems, springs engaged on each sleeve and against the ends of the valve stems and acting to hold the valves seated, cam actuated rocker arms extending outwardly along each side of each cylinder with the longer arms thereof contacting a valve stem, and the shorter ends thereof in position to be contacted by the appropriate cam on the cam shaft, said mechanisms being in open communication with the crank case for splash lubrication, and a cover plate wholly inclosing said mechanisms within the casing of the engine.

4. In a device of the class described the combination with an internal combustion engine and its crank case extended at one side of the engine and open for its entire length, of a valve gear therefor comprising a cam shaft in said crank case driven from the crank shaft of the engine, a tubular shaft mounted above said cam shaft, a plurality of rocker arms journaled on said tubular shaft, with the lower ends thereof extending inwardly into the crank case through the open portion thereof, ports in said shafts to permit oil to flow from the interior of said shaft to the bearing for said rocker arms, valves mounted at the upper ends of the cylinders adapted to be actuated by said rocker arms, and a pipe mounted on each rocker arm leading from the bearings in said rocker arms to the point of contact of the rocker arms and cam shafts to admit lubricating oil thereto.

5. The combination with an internal combustion engine and its crank case, of valves communicating laterally in spaces above each of the cylinders of the engine, rocker arms projecting into said crank case for opening said valves, springs for returning said valves to closed position, a cam shaft in the crank case driven from the crank shaft of the engine for actuating said rocker arms, an oil pump, mechanism on said cam shaft for operating the same, communication between said oil pump and the supports for said rocker arms, whereby oil is forced into the interior of said supports and fed outwardly therethrough into the bearings of each of said rocker arms, and a pipe secured on each of the rocker arms and movable therewith adapted to transmit oil from said supports to said mechanism on the cam shaft.

6. In a valve gear for internal combustion engines a stationary tubular shaft, a plu-

rality of rocker arms journaled thereon, ports in said shaft and rocker arms adapted to register with one another, a cam shaft for actuating said rocker arms, a pipe connected rigidly on each of said rocker arms and movable therewith and communicating with the port in the rocker arm and at its other end adapted to discharge oil received from said tubular shaft through the registering ports to the contacting surfaces of the rocker arm and cam shaft, and valves for the engine adapted to be actuated by said rocker arms.

In testimony whereof we have hereunto subscribed our names in the presence of two subscribing witnesses.

FREDERICK S. DUESENBERG.
AUGUST S. DUESENBERG.

Witnesses to signature of August S. Duesenberg:
    CHARLES W. HILLS, Jr.,
    FRANK K. HUDSON.

Witnesses to signature of Frederick S. Duesenberg:
    E. A. SLININGER,
    WRAY BERTHOLF.

Levett Pistons ad from late January 1919 with a letter from Fred Duesenberg thanking the company for their pistons. Most likely, Levett Magnalite aluminum pistons were used in all Duesenberg aircraft engines.

Appendix C – The King V-12 Aero Engine

According to *The Bulletin of the Airplane Engineering Department*, the Duesenberg Motors Corporation was contracted to build five prototypes of the King V-12 aero engine. This contract lasted only briefly, from late June 1918 to mid-October 1918.

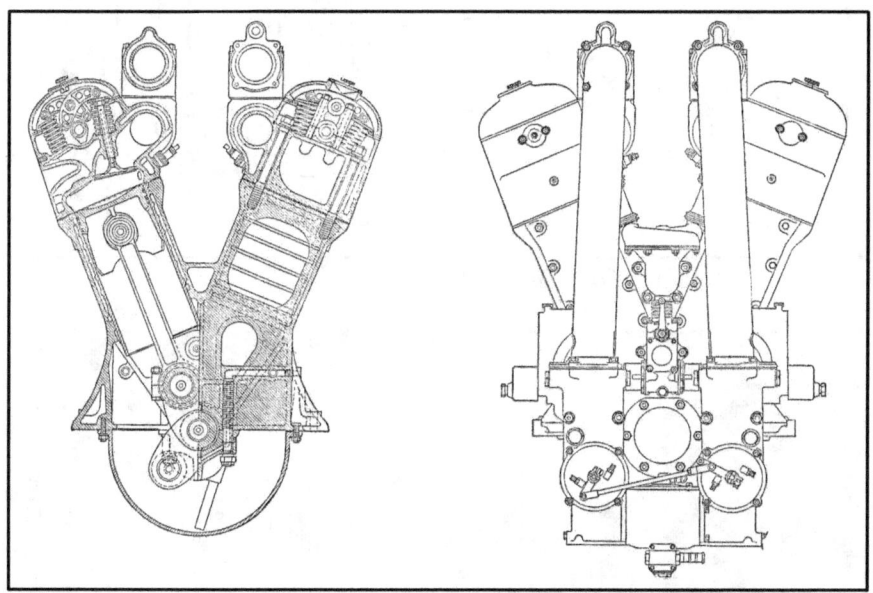

Front sectional view and rear end view of the King V-12 engine.

Designed by Charles B. King, the King aero engine was a 45° V-12 engine. With a bore of 5 1/2" and a stroke of 7", the engine displaced 1,995 in^3. A gear reduction of 0.692:1 was fitted, and the engine was rated at 500 hp at 1,700 rpm (1,175 rpm at the propeller); 550 hp at 1,880 rpm (1,300 rpm at the propeller); and 600 hp at 2,075 rpm (1,435 rpm at the propeller). The compression ratio was 5:1, and the engine weighed 990 lb dry. The engine was intended as a Liberty V-12 replacement and could be installed in place of the Liberty engine. King's V-12 was a compact design and had less frontal area than the Liberty.

The engine was of all aluminum, monobloc construction and featured three valves per cylinder. The one intake and two exhaust valves for each cylinder were actuated by a single overhead camshaft. The head for each bank of six cylinders was cast complete, and the valve gear was enclosed

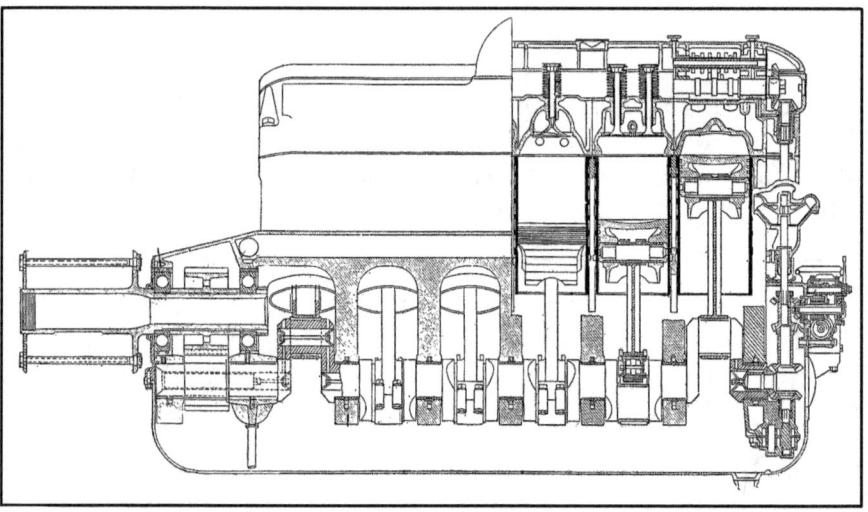

Sectional side view of the King V-12.

Various pieces of the King V-12, including a cylinder head, engine case (bottom view), valves, rockers, and a camshaft. Note the sectioned head on the left and the carburetor on the far right.

by a valve cover. Each camshaft was driven by a vertical shaft mounted at the rear of the engine casting. These vertical shafts had bevel gears at their top and bottom, were driven by the crankshaft, and were each enclosed by a cover to which a magneto was mounted.

The cylinder blocks were aluminum castings, machined inside and out, and had a press-fit cast iron liner 1/16" in wall thickness. Non-ribbed aluminum pistons with five rings were used. The connecting rods were

Front view of a partially assembled King V-12 highlighting its all-aluminum, cast construction. Note the spark plug fitted to one of the rear cylinders.

the articulated type. The articulated pin was 45° from the center line of the master rod and was supported on tapered split rings clamped into lugs on the master rod. The crankshaft was supported by eight main bearings.

The two King-designed carburetors were mounted under the magnetos, and each carburetor fed one cylinder bank. Two spark plugs per cylinder were fired by two Dixie magnetos running at crankshaft speed.

A pressure oiling system was used with a normal running pressure of 45 psi. A scavenge pump and a pressure oil pump were located in one housing bolted to the rear main bearing cap. The pumps were driven from the same shaft by bevel gears from the crankshaft. The scavenging pump drew oil from the propeller end of the crankcase and delivered it to the oil tank, which was separate from the engine. Another pipe led from the rear of the crankcase to the oil tank. The oil flowed through this pipe by gravity to the oil tank. This system was first used by Charles King on the King-Bugatti engine. The engine had no external oil piping. All oil passages were either cast or machined into the various parts, making it impossible for any oil connection to become loose during operation.

Once Charles King was assigned to work on the Bugatti engine, work on his own engine was continued at the Brewster and Company plant in Long Island, NY. From the beginning of April 1918, the Aeronautical Engineering Corporation, also in Long Island, was contracted to construct five complete engines and spare parts. This contract was transferred to the Duesenberg Motors Corporation in late June. It is not known how much work progressed on the engine, but this engine was given much lower priority than the King-Bugatti. In October 1918, work on the engines was stopped, and Duesenberg sent all parts to the Airplane Engineering Division at McCook Field in Dayton, Ohio. Duesenberg had 56 boxes of parts delivered to McCook field on November 15, 1918, but work on the engine essentially stopped after the Armistice.

Appendix D – Duesenberg Engine Test House

In February of 1918, ground was broken for the Duesenberg engine test house in Elizabeth, NJ; its purpose was to test experimental and production engines. This expansion was due to World War I and the various engine contracts the Duesenberg Motors Corporation was involved with, mainly the contract to build 2,000 King-Bugatti engines.

The test house building was completed in May of 1918 and was 240' by 67'. Inside the building was an oil filter room as well as a chemical and a

The Duesenberg engine test house in the background with the 75,000 gallon cooling water fountain in the foreground. Visible are the two 85 foot exhaust stacks.

physical testing laboratory. The laboratories were equipped with the most modern equipment and instruments to fully analyze every aspect of the Duesenberg engines.

The main test room was 176' long and 67' wide. Twenty–two engines could be tested simultaneously because each stand had its own fuel and oil supply. The fuel supply tanks were on scales so that careful consumption measurements could be taken, and the oil tanks had calibrated sight gauges. The supply tanks were replenished from main tanks via electric pumps.

A worker with a large test club stands next to an empty engine test stand. This appears to be the same propeller used on the Model H engine.

While each test stand had its own water tank, all the tanks were connected to a circulating system driven by an electric pump. Hot water was taken away from the engine and test house to a cooling fountain outside. This concrete fountain was 50' in diameter and had a cooling capacity of 75,000 gallons. Exhaust gases from each engine were directed through main ducts beneath the floor and then carried outside through two 85' vertical stacks that vented the exhaust and also muffled the noise.

Appendix D – Duesenberg Engine Test House

Once an engine was completed in the factory, it was taken to the test house via a special truck that delivered it to the test stand. The truck was backed up to the stand, and the motor was lifted into place. During testing, recording thermometers automatically measured the temperatures of water and oil as they entered and exited the engine.

The dynamometer testing room with the three Sprague dynamometers in the foreground. The Model H is attached to the dyno at the far left.

A Sprague Electric ad from 1919 showcasing the Duesenberg engine test house and referencing the 800 hp of the Model H engine.

A special dynamometer testing room was used for horsepower tests. This room housed three 300-400 horsepower Sprague Electric dynamometers that could handle a maximum of 3,500 rpm. Test clubs used on production engines were calibrated on a sample engine hooked up to the dynamometer brake. All experimental power tests were run on the dynamometers. The three dynamometers were arranged in tandem and could be coupled together for maximum dynamometer braking when testing high-powered engines. Although the dynamometers were never used in this capacity, their output could have provided enough electricity to power the entire Duesenberg plant.

The Duesenberg site, including the factory and engine test house, was sold to the Willys Corporation in late 1919. The Willys Corporation was a separate entity than Willys-Overland, even though John Willys was in charge of both companies. By 1920, the Duesenberg plant was demolished to make way for a new factory, six times larger, to produce Willys automobiles.

Another Sprague Electric ad from 1919, this time featuring the King-Bugatti engine. This appears to be the same photo of the Model H under testing as seen on page 73 but with an image of the King-Bugatti superimposed over the Model H.

Appendix E – Christensen Self-Starter

Both the Duesenberg 16-valve, four-cylinder engine and the Model H used Christensen self-starters. The Christensen self-starter was a novel solution to overcome some of the starting issues that troubled early engines. Swinging the propeller by hand was always a dangerous and ineffective way to start large aircraft engines.

The starter was designed by Niels Anton Christensen, an engineer specializing in pneumatics, and built by the Christensen Engineering Company out of Milwaukee, Wisconsin. The Christensen starter was composed of an air compressor, a carburetor, and an automatic distributor with one valve for each cylinder.

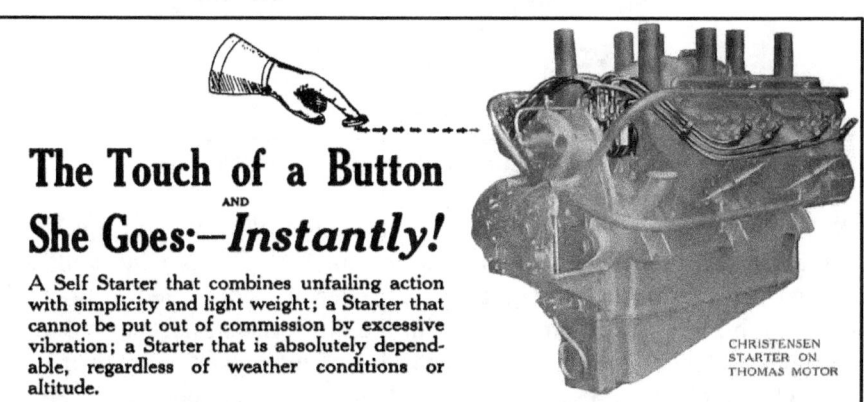

Christensen self-starter ad from 1917.

The air compressor stored pressurized air in a tank located in the aircraft fuselage. A three position control valve in the cockpit governed the operation of the starter. The first position was for starting the engine; the second cut off air to the starter but allowed air from the tank to be used for tire inflation; and the third was for operating the compressor, when the engine was running, to fill the air tank. A button controlled cutout valve opened the line between the control valve and the air tank, allowing air to flow from the tank to the starter or to the tank from the compressor, depending on the position of the control valve.

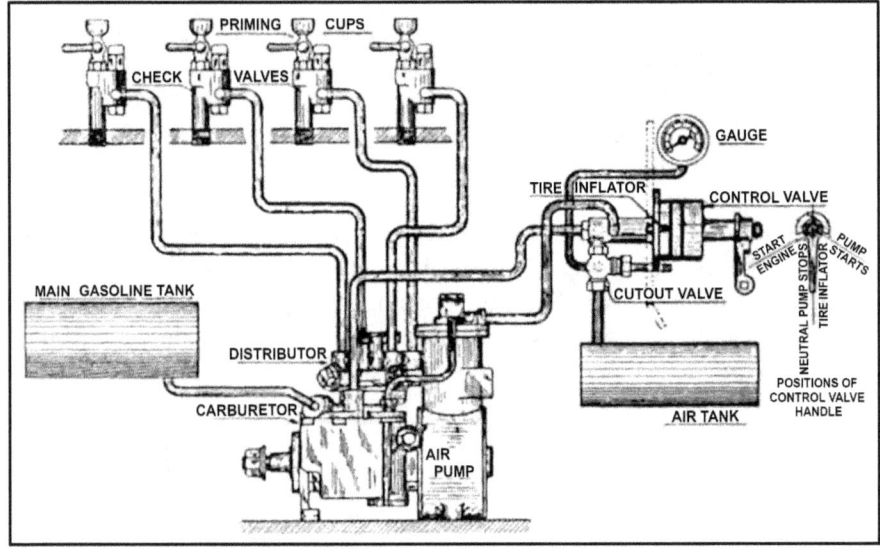

Schematic showing the components of the Christensen self-starter.

When "Start Engine" was selected on the control valve and the cutout valve button was depressed, pressurized air flowed from the tank to a special carburetor that was part of the starter and connected to the main fuel supply. Fuel was then mixed with the air in the starter and fed to the distributor. A cam driven from the engine opened valves in the distributor through which the pressurized air/fuel mixture was sent to the engine cylinders by firing order. Once the air/fuel mixture entered the cylinder, it simulated the compression stroke, and the rich mixture was ignited by the spark plug. This process was repeated in the other cylinders by firing order until the engine began to run on its own. A check valve in the lead to each cylinder prevented a backfire into the distributor.

The air compressor was a single-cylinder, single-acting type driven by any shaft on the engine. Through a clutch, the compressor could be completely disconnected from the engine. A gauge in the cockpit indicated the air pressure in the tank, which should have been kept between 225 and 250 psi.

All parts on the starter were made of aluminum and chrome vanadium steel, heat treated and ground to a perfect fit. The starter was automatically lubricated using oil from the engine and was predicted to outlive the engine it was installed on. The Christensen self-starter had no wiring or storage batteries. The complete unit weighed about 40 lb.

During a test on a Hall-Scott engine, the air tank was filled to 250 psi, and 28 complete starts were made without recharging. The last start was made with a tank pressure of 100 psi. The starter was used on aircraft engines manufactured by Duesenberg, Curtiss, Hall-Scott, Sturtevant, Thomas, Wisconsin, and others. It was also used on automobiles, trucks, tractors, and boats.

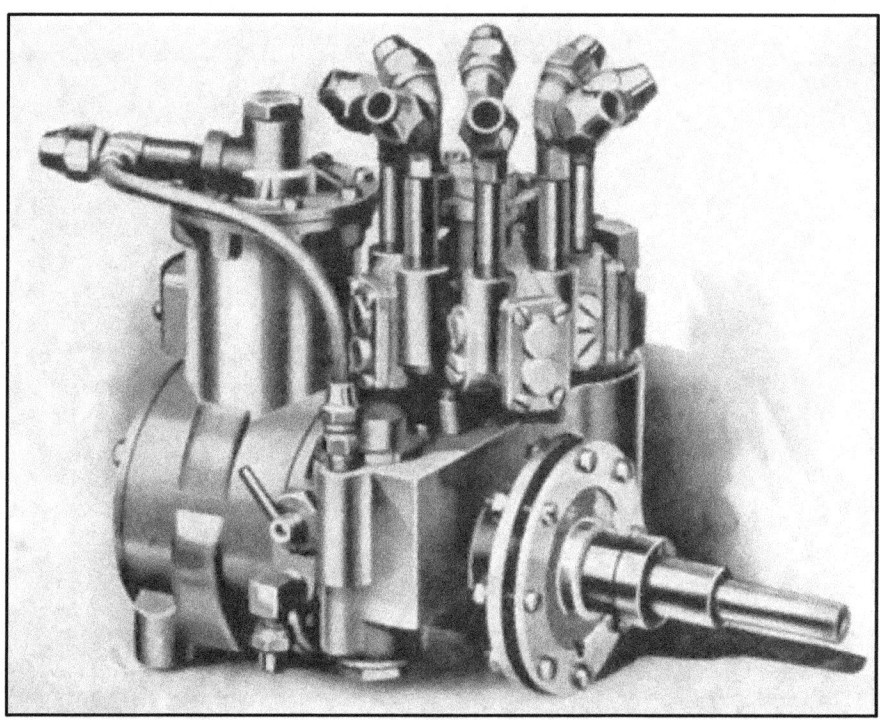

The compressor and distributor of the Christensen self-starter.

It is interesting to note that N. A. Christensen, through his work on pneumatics and air brakes, went on to perfect the O-ring in the 1930s and was granted United States patent 2,180,795 in 1939 for the invention.

Duesenberg tribute ad from 1919 thanking all the equipment manufacturers who made building engines possible.

Appendix F – Notes on Descriptions and Conflicting Information

I generally prefer decimals over fractions. However, for readability and to present figures in the simplest way possible, fractions were a better alternative, especially when dealing with numbers like 63/64. I used fractions throughout the text but used decimals for the engine specifications and comparison chart.

I used the terms "left" and "right" several times to describe which side of the engine various engine parts and equipment were located. In reference to this, the view is from standing behind the engine, where the front of the engine (propeller end) is farthest from view, and the rear of the engine (no propeller) is closest.

During my research, I occasionally found different figures for the same engine. Some of these discrepancies were simply different power/rpm combinations between a direct drive engine and a geared drive engine, both turning a fixed pitch propeller at the same speed. But conflicting information extended beyond the engines. For example, many cannot agree on whether F. Duesenberg's first name was spelled Frederick, Frederic, Fredrick, Friedrich, etc. I tried to include only factual information, but unfortunately, some mistakes may have been repeated.

In my humble opinion, the images of the first Duesenberg aircraft engines, the Special A and the Special A3, look much more automotive than they do aeronautic. In fact, they are remarkably similar to the engine illustrated in the Duesenberg *Internal Combustion Engine* and *Valve Gear* patents of 1913 and 1914, respectively. I have to wonder if images of these engines were originally referenced in publications as examples of Duesenberg engines rather than as engines designed specifically for use in aircraft. Since images of these engines have made their way into many publications as aircraft engines, and since I cannot say they were not aircraft engines, I have included them in this book. However, I have not found any other images of these engines or any references to aircraft that they powered or were proposed to power.

The Special A and Special A3 were referred to by name in an article and a Duesenberg ad, both from May 1915. Considering the source, an ad from the manufacturer, I too referred to the engines as the Special A and Special A3. Angle, in *Airplane Engine Encyclopedia* from 1921, refers to an engine of the same specifications as the Special A3, but called A-44. This is repeated in Angle's *Aerosphere 1939* and is subsequently repeated in later works by various authors. Outside of Angle and later works based on his, I have not found a reference to any A-44 engine. However, I found at least one reference to the 16-valve, four-cylinder engine being called the A-4.

Engine names were not the only source of confusion; engine specifications were often inconsistent as well. Some authors have combined specifications of the Special A3 of 1915 and the 16-valve, four-cylinder of 1916, referring to this "hybrid" as the A-44. I can only assume they were under the impression that only one four-cylinder engine was made and that any figures regarding a four-cylinder must belong to that one engine.

Duesenberg built a special marine straight 12-cylinder engine of 750 hp, two of which were installed in James Pugh's *Disturber IV* motorboat in 1914. This is the 12-cylinder engine included in *All the World's Aircraft 1916*, not the V-12 aircraft engine that Duesenberg built in 1916. The aircraft V-12 has occasionally been referred to as a 45° Vee, but it was a 60°. At least one source referred to Schebler carburetors being used on the V-12, but most sources listed Miller carburetors. Most sources stated the bore as 4 7/8", which I have repeated. However, a few sources listed the bore as 4 3/4", which would give a total displacement of 1,488 in^3.

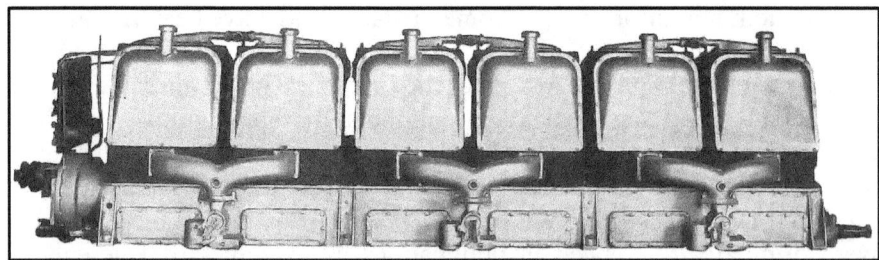

The Duesenberg straight 12-cylinder marine engine of 3,221 in^3 capacity and 750 hp. Two of these engines were installed in the Disturber IV *motorboat, the first boat clocked at over 60 mph.*

The King-Bugatti's true weight was hard to pin down. Numbers vary from 1,000 lb to 1,286 lb, and strangely, articles from the era often omitted the weight entirely or did not give the weight of the complete engine. An engine weight of 1,248 lb dry and an additional 38 lb with water in the jackets matches the 1,286 lb given by most modern sources, such as the National Air and Space Museum.

Horsepower ratings for the King-Bugatti varied from 400 hp to 420 hp, but typically a number of 410 hp at 2,000 rpm is given. Because the focus of this work is on Duesenberg aircraft engines, and since the King-Bugatti engine was not of Duesenberg design, I chose not to describe it in as much detail as the other engines.

As for the Model H, most sources say there were four prototype engines. However, *The Bulletin of the Airplane Engineering Department* stated that the original contract of April 1918 was for two geared drive engines, but this contract was changed in June of 1918 to one geared drive engine and one direct drive engine. The Bulletin makes no mention of more than two 16-cylinder Duesenberg Model H engines being built, but it is possible that an additional two engines were built for the Navy.

Horsepower ratings for the Model H varied widely, from 700 hp to 900 hp. Most sources settled on 800 hp in reference to the geared version, but some listed 800 hp in one place and 850 hp in another. It seems the higher numbers were either obtained or thought to be obtainable at engine speeds above 1,800 rpm. For the direct drive version, 700 hp was a common figure.

The "Duesenberg Sixteen-Cylinder Aircraft Engine" article from *Automotive Industries* dated January 23, 1917 was the source of the oil pressure information for the Model H engine. The article stated that a low pressure line was taken off from the main oil distributing line, and oil pressure was reduced to "2/8" psi. This is oddly written and seems low. I did not include this figure in the engine description but wanted to include it here for reference.

Again, it is not my intention to repeat incorrect information, but I'm sure that this is unavoidable. I hope that someday someone will pick up where I left off and complete a definitive/authoritative history of Duesenberg aircraft engines. These obscure, forgotten engines and the people who created them deserved to be remembered.

Duesenberg ad from 1919.

Bibliography

Angelucci, Enzo, and Peter Bowers. *The American Fighter*. Orion Books, 1987.
Angle, Glenn D. *Aerosphere 1939*. Aircraft Publications, 1940.
Angle, Glenn D. *Airplane Engine Encyclopedia*. Otterbein Press, 1921.
Angle, Glenn D. "Progress Toward 1000 Hp. Aircraft Engines." *Aviation*. 25 February 1924.
Borgeson, Griffith. *The Golden Age of the American Racing Car (Second Edition)*. Society of Automotive Engineers, 1998.
The Bulletin of the Airplane Engineering Department Vol. 1 & 2. Bureau of Aircraft Production, 1918.
"The Christensen Self-Starter for Aerial Motors." *Aerial Age Weekly*. 14 February 1916.
Clupper, Martt. "1919 Duesenberg Model H: V-16 Aircraft Engine." *AirPigz*. 13 February 2010, http://airpigz.com/blog/2010/2/13/1919-duesenberg-model-h-v-16-aircraft-engine-amazing.html.
De Seta, Tony. "The Power of the Hour." *The Old Motor*. 16 January 2011, http://theoldmotor.com/?p=1832.
Dickey, Philip S., III. *The Liberty Engine 1918-1942*. Smithsonian Institution Press, 1968.
"The Duesenberg Aero Engine." *Aerial Age Weekly*. 29 January 1917.
"The Duesenberg Aero Engine." *Aviation and Aeronautical Engineering*. 15 September 1916.
Duesenberg, F.S. and A.S. Duesenberg. *Internal Combustion Engine*. Patent 1,363,500. 28 December 1920.
Duesenberg, F.S. and A.S. Duesenberg. *Valve Gear*. Patent 1,244,481. 30 October 1917.
"Duesenberg Historical Highlights." *Keith Duesenberg & Leik Motorsports*. http://www.duesenberg-racing.com/historyauto.htm.
"The Duesenberg Model H." *Aerial Age Weekly*. 3 March 1919.
"Duesenberg Motors Corp. v. United States - 260 U.S. 115 (1922)." *Justia.com US Supreme Court Center*. http://supreme.justia.com/cases/federal/us/260/115/case.html.
"Duesenberg Sixteen-Cylinder Aircraft Engine." *Automotive Industries*. 23 January 1919.
"Fred S. Duesenberg, Pioneer High Duty Engine Builder." *Aerial Age Weekly*. 25 November 1918.
Gordon, Robert A. "The Gallaudet D-1 and the Gallaudet Drive Aircraft." *The Early Birds of Aviation, Inc.* http://earlyaviators.com/ebjorkl1.htm.

Greenlees, David. "The Duesenberg V-12 Aircraft Engine." *The Old Motor.* 8 July 2011, http://theoldmotor.com/?p=23344.
Greenlees, David. "The Incredible V-16 Duesenberg Engine." *The Old Motor.* 9 July 2011, http://theoldmotor.com/?p=23469.
Greenlees, David. "Sixteen Valves." *The Old Motor.* 14 June 2011, http://theoldmotor.com/?p=20330.
Grey, C.G. *All the World's Aircraft 1916.* Sampson Low, 1916.
Grey, C.G. *All the World's Aircraft 1917.* Sampson Low, 1917.
Grey, C.G. *All the World's Aircraft 1918.* Sampson Low, 1918.
Grey, C.G. *All the World's Aircraft 1919.* Sampson Low, 1919.
Hourwich, Iskander and W.J.Foster. *Air Service Engine Handbook.* Engineering Division U.S. Army Air Service, 1925.
"King-Bugatti 16-Cylinder Aero Engine" (Part I). *Automotive Industries.* 24 April 1919.
"King-Bugatti 16-Cylinder Aero Engine" (Part II). *Automotive Industries.* 1 May 1919.
"The King 550 Hp. Aircraft Engine." *Aviation and Aeronautical Engineering.* 1 April 1919.
Knappen, Theodore Macfarlane. *Wings of War.* G. P. Putnam's Sons, 1920.
Lewis, W. David. *Eddie Rickenbacker.* Johns Hopkins University Press, 2005.
"The M.F.P. Tractor Biplane." *Flight.* 15 June 1916.
MacCoull, N. "Duesenberg Motors." *Aerial Age Weekly.* 10 May 1915.
Molson, K.M. and H.A. Taylor. *Canadian Aircraft Since 1909.* Putnam, 1982.
Neal, Robert J. *The Engineering Division W-1.* Aircraft Engine Historical Society, 2009.
Neal, Robert J. *Master Motor Builders.* Aero-Marine History Publishing Company, 2000.
"The New Duesenberg Aero Engine Test House." *Aerial Age Weekly.* 23 September 1918.
"Orenco Commercial and Military Types." *Aerial Age Weekly.* 29 March 1920.
Page, Victor W. *Aviation Engines.* Norman Henley Publishing Company, 1917.
Sherbondy, E.H., and G. Douglas Wardrop. *Textbook of Aero Engines.* Fredrick A. Stokes Company, 1920.
Skinner, Sandy. "The U-16 Revisited." *Torque Meter: Journal of the Aircraft Engine Historical Society Vol. 5 No. 3*, Summer 2006.
Smith, Herschel. *Aircraft Piston Engines.* McGraw-Hill Inc., 1981.
Smyth, Ross. *The Lindbergh of Canada: The Erroll Boyd Story.* General Store Publishing House, 1997.
"Some American Aero Engines: The Duesenberg." *Flight.* 10 September 1915.
Wagner, Ray. *American Combat Planes of the 20th Century.* Jack Bacon & Co., 2004.
Wardrop, Douglas G. "The Duesenberg Model H 850 H.P. Motor." *Aerial Age Weekly.* 27 January 1919.
Wardrop, Douglas G. "The King-Bugatti Aviation Engine" (Part I). *Aerial Age Weekly.* 10 February 1919.
Wardrop, Douglas G. "The King-Bugatti Aviation Motor" (Part II). *Aerial Age Weekly.* 17 February 1919.